Contents

As we live in a rapidly changing society, exposure to and fluency in Science, Technology, Engineering, and Mathematics (STEM) ensures students will gain the skills they will need to succeed in the 21st century. It is essential that students gain practice in becoming good problem solvers, critical thinkers, innovators, inventors, and risk takers.

Teacher Tips

Encourage Topic Interest

Help students develop an understanding and appreciation of different STEM concepts by providing an area in the classroom to display topic-related non-fiction books, pictures, collections, and artifacts as a springboard for learning.

What I Think I Know / What I Would Like to Know Activity

Introduce each STEM unit by asking students what they think they know about the topic, and what they would like to know about the topic. Complete this activity as a whole-group brainstorming session, in cooperative small groups, or independently. Once students have had a chance to complete the questions, combine the information to create a class chart for display. Throughout the study, periodically update students' progress in accomplishing their goal of what they want to know, and validate what they think they know.

Vocabulary List

Keep track of new and content-related vocabulary on chart paper for students' reference. Encourage students to add words to the list. Classify the word list into the categories of nouns, verbs, and adjectives. In addition, have students create their own science dictionaries as part of their learning logs.

Learning Logs

Keeping a learning log is an effective way for students to organize thoughts and ideas about the STEM concepts presented and examined. Students' learning logs also provide insight on what follow-up activities are needed to review and to clarify concepts learned.

Learning logs can include the following types of entries:

- Teacher prompts
- Students' personal reflections
- Questions that arise
- Connections discovered
- Labeled diagrams and pictures
- Definitions for new vocabulary

Living Things

You know that our world is made up of living and non-living things. A bird is a living thing. A rock is not. But what makes something alive? We are alive, but so is a tree. What do we have in common with a tree?

Characteristics of Living Things

Living things are called organisms. All organisms share certain characteristics:

- **Organisms are made up of one or more cells.** Cells are the basic unit of life. They are the smallest unit of living matter. Some organisms, such as bacteria, have just one cell. They are unicellular. Other organisms, such as humans, have many cells. They are multicellular.

- **Organisms use materials and energy from their environment to grow and develop.** Humans eat food. With the help of water, their bodies turn the food into energy. Green plants use sunlight and water to make their own food for energy.

- **Organisms respond to their environment.** A cat might respond to a loud sound by running away. Flowers respond to sunlight by turning toward the Sun.

- **Organisms respire.** This means they exchange gases with their environment. Animals and humans breathe in air (oxygen) and breathe out carbon dioxide. Plants do the opposite when they are making food. They take in carbon dioxide and release oxygen.

- **Organisms reproduce.** They can produce copies of themselves. Bacteria reproduce by splitting in two. Some plants reproduce through seeds. Some animals lay eggs. Other animals give birth to live young.

Needs of Living Things

To stay alive, organisms must meet their needs. These needs include food and water to get the energy they need to grow, develop, and reproduce. They need air to get the gases they need. They need the right place to live (habitat) that provides everything they need to stay alive.

1. Choose an organism that you know a lot about. You might choose an animal such as a rabbit, or a plant such as a potato plant. On a separate piece of paper, write a paragraph explaining how you know your choice is a living thing.

2. Look at the chart below.

a) Write what each item is made of.   b) Circle the items that are living.

Item	Made out of
rock	
cheese	
paper	
wool scarf	
glass jar	

3. Choose an animal that lives in your environment. Explain how the animal meets its needs for food and water.

____

____

____

____

____

____

4. Temperature is important to living things. Some organisms can survive where the temperature is very hot. Some can survive where the temperature is very cold. Is temperature part of what living things need? Why?

____

____

____

____

____

____

Classifying Organisms

There are many types of life on Earth. All living things share certain characteristics, so they all belong to one group: organisms. Scientists believe there are over 10 million types of organisms on Earth. Classifying organisms helps scientists study them and understand them better.

Characteristics are used to classify an organism. Characteristics include what the parts of the organism do. What the organism looks like on the inside and outside is another characteristic.

The most common classification system divides organisms into five kingdoms: Plantae, Animalia, Fungi, Monera, and Protista. Within each kingdom, organisms are divided into smaller groups. Within those groups, they are divided into even smaller groups. As the groups are divided further, the organisms become more alike. There are more similarities in plants in the same family than in plants in the same phylum.

Kingdom

Phylum

Class

Order

Family

Genus

Species

"Classifying Organisms"—Think About It!

1. Why do you think this classification system changed since the 1700s?

____

____

2. Why is it important for all scientists to use the same classification system?

____

____

3. You have six animals to classify in the flowchart below: sea star, squirrel, lion, trout, whale, and sparrow. Use common characteristics to categorize the first group into two groups. Then divide each group into two groups. Keep dividing groups until you have only one animal in a category. (You may not need to use all the boxes.) In each box, write the characteristic you are using to classify the animals, then the name of the animals. For example, one classification may be "Has fur: lion, squirrel" and "Does not have fur: sparrow."

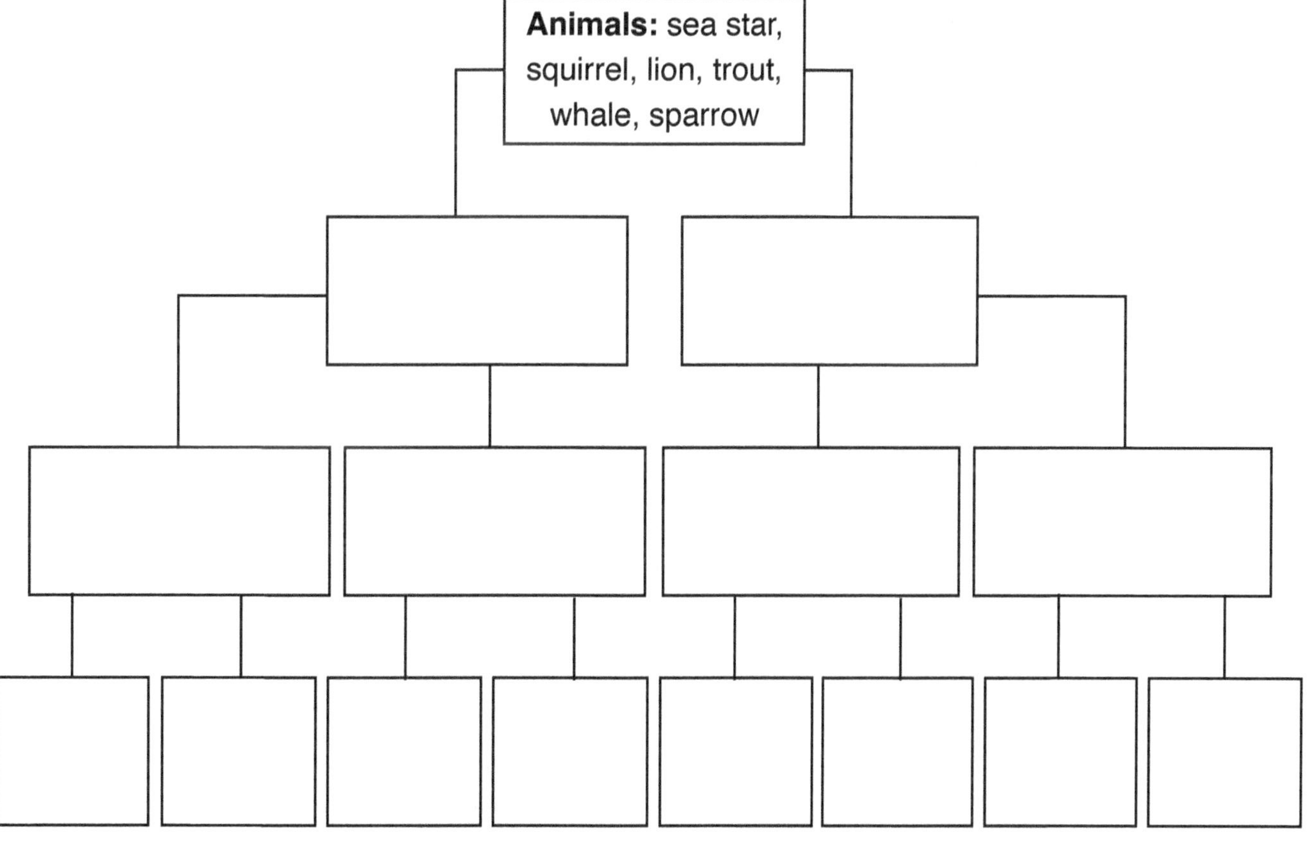

The Animal Kingdom

All animals share these characteristics:

- multicellular
- rely on other organisms for food
- can move around or move parts of their bodies to get food
- most need two individuals to reproduce

All animals can be divided into two main groups: vertebrates and invertebrates. Vertebrates have a spinal cord surrounded by a backbone. Invertebrates do not. All vertebrates are in the phylum Chordata, which includes amphibians, reptiles, birds, fish, and mammals. Invertebrates are divided into many phyla (the plural of phylum). These include annelids (worms), and mollusks such as snails and clams. The phylum Arthropod has sub-phyla that contain insects, crustaceans, and arachnids.

Only about 5 percent of animals are vertebrates. How much do you know about invertebrates?

Characteristics of Invertebrates

Phylum/Sub-phylum	Examples	Characteristics
Insects	• butterfly • ant • grasshopper • fly	• six jointed legs • three body parts • almost all have wings • exoskeleton (outer skeleton)
Arachnids	• spider • scorpion • tick • mite	• usually eight jointed legs • exoskeleton • two body sections • lay eggs
Crustaceans	• crab • lobster • barnacle	• exoskeleton • two body parts • jointed legs or claws • two pairs of antennae
Annelids	• earthworm • flatworm • leech	• segmented bodies • no limbs • most are covered with short bristles
Mollusks	• snail • octopus • oyster	• soft body • either external or internal shell • some have a single foot used for moving, attaching to things, or getting food, while others have eight or more tentacles

"The Animal Kingdom"—Think About It!

1. Explain why a bullfrog is an animal.

____

____

2. Why do you think humans are more familiar with vertebrates than with other animals?

____

____

3. Why are insects, arachnids, and crustaceans in the same phylum?

____

____

4. What do insects have that makes them different from other invertebrates?

____

____

5. Complete the web below by adding the characteristics of each class of vertebrates.
Use what you know, and check references if necessary. Try to add at least three for each.
Share your web with a classmate. Do you agree with each other's characteristics?

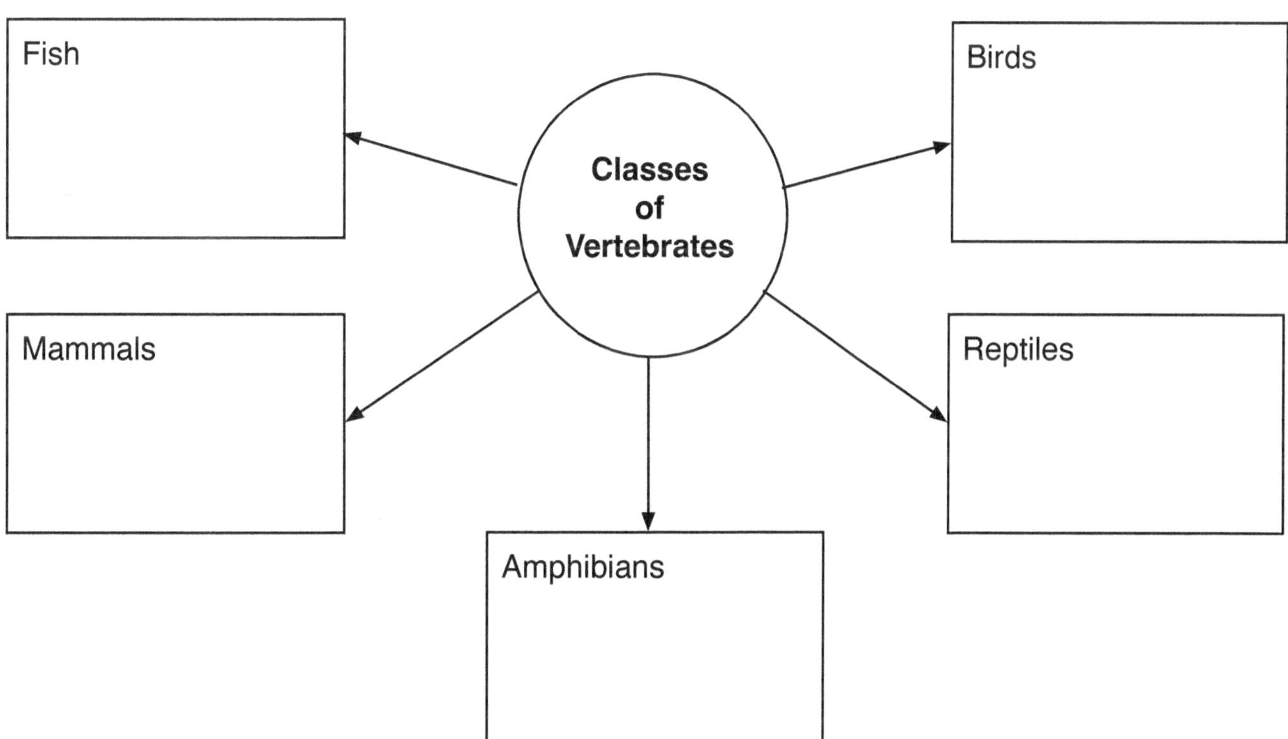

The Forgotten Kingdoms

People rarely think about organisms in the Monera, Protista, and Fungi kingdoms.

The Monera Kingdom

- only one cell
- most simple cell structure
- reproduce by splitting in two
- most absorb nutrients from outside their bodies

Bacteria are everywhere. They turn milk into yogurt and cheese. They help decompose waste. They can keep us healthy or make us sick. They are used to produce many medicines that treat diseases. Although we cannot see them, bacteria are very important in our lives.

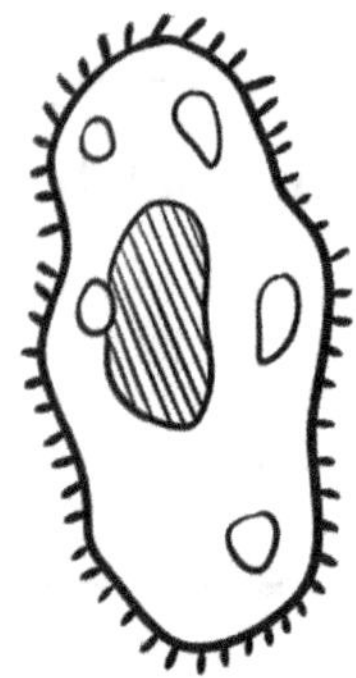

bacteria

The Protista Kingdom

- do not fit in any other kingdom
- not bacteria, fungi, plants, or animals
- most have only one cell
- more complex cell structure than monerans
- live mostly in water, but can survive in moist soil and inside animals
- most reproduce by splitting in two

Protists are classified according to how they move and how they get nutrition. So there are animal-like protists, plant-like protists, and fungus-like protists. Algae are plant-like protists. They produce their own food. Amoebas are animal-like protists. They consume other organisms for food. Drinking water that contains certain types of amoebas can make people sick. Slime molds are fungus-like protists. They absorb nutrients from their environment.

algae

continued next page

The Fungi Kingdom

- many cells
- get nutrients from dead plants and animals
- decomposers that help turn dead organisms into nutrients that make soil rich

Fungi are used to produce many medicines. We eat some types of fungi. Yeast is a fungus used for baking. Some fungi can cause infections, such as athlete's foot and ringworm. Others can damage crops.

mushroom

Think About It!

1. Summarize what you have learned about the Monera, Protista, and Fungi kingdoms. Decide on the categories of information. Write those as column headings. For example, you could use "Cells" and "Getting Nutrition" as headings. You can research these kingdoms to find the information you need.

Monera					
Protista					
Fungi					

Cells: The Building Blocks of All Organisms

Did you know that cells are the building blocks of all organisms on Earth? All living organisms are made up of tiny parts called cells. A cell is the smallest part of an organism, but this tiny part holds everything needed to carry out actions to keep the organism alive. Cells take in nutrients and turn them into energy. They also get rid of wastes, do work, and reproduce. Cells are vital!

Organisms made up of only one cell are unicellular. For example, an amoeba is a unicellular organism that is very tiny. It can only grow to a certain size and cannot be seen with the naked eye. Organisms made up of more than one cell are multicellular. For example, humans are multicellular and can grow to different sizes. People have trillions of cells!

Cell Parts

Cells are classified into either plant or animal cells. Plant and animal cells are very similar and contain most of the same parts. All cells are filled with a jelly-like fluid called cytoplasm. This fluid contains many chemicals that help the cell stay alive. In addition, every cell has a cell membrane that keeps the cytoplasm inside. The cell membrane also keeps the parts of the cell together. Most cells have a nucleus, which is the cell's command center. The nucleus directs the cell's actions and contains the DNA. DNA is the genetic material that lets cells reproduce themselves. It also lets them pass their traits on to new cells.

How Do We See Cells?

A microscope is needed to see most cells clearly. A light microscope can help you see bacteria and their structures, including the nucleus. The best microscope is the electron microscope. With it, you can see things much smaller than a cell.

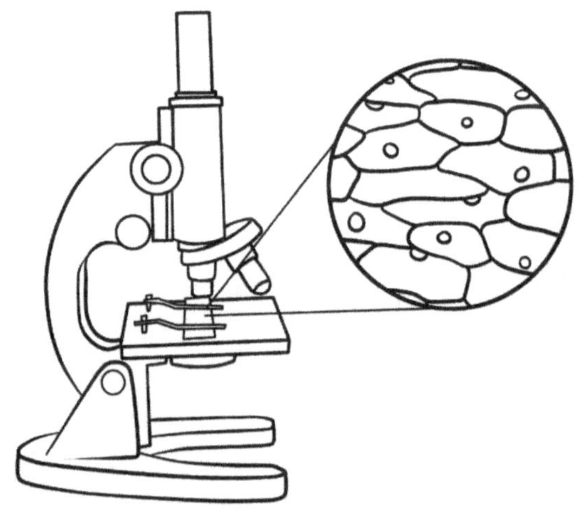

light microscope

1. Is it correct to compare a cell to the human body? Explain your thinking.

____

____

____

____

____

____

____

____

2. Create a web to organize what you have learned about cells

Biodiversity

Scientists estimate that there are 1.7 million species of animals and plants in the world. This means that there is amazing diversity of life on our planet. Most species tend to live in specific areas, or habitats. In these habitats, they can find the things they need to stay alive.

Classifications of Habitats

Scientists classify habitats the same way they classify organisms: by their characteristics. Scientists have not agreed on one system of classification for habitats. But all systems used are based on similar plant, animal, and climatic features. The systems start with large groups that are further divided into smaller and smaller groups.

The largest groups of habitats are biomes. There are many types of biomes. Examples include deserts, forests, grasslands, tundra, and oceans. Each of these groups is divided into smaller groups. For example, the forest groups include boreal, subarctic, subtropical, and temperate.

Scientists study organisms in smaller areas to better understand them. They study how the organisms interact with each other and with the environment. The environment includes non-living things such as soil, water, air, heat, and light. A habitat community is made up of the set of organisms that live within a certain area. The area could be as large as a forest, or as small as a pond.

Why Is Biodiversity Important?

Each species, no matter how small, has a role to play. A healthy community of diverse species will be able to sustain life. The species are better able to recover from natural disasters and changes in climate.

Our quality of life depends on biodiversity. We get many things from our environment. These include food products, timber, fresh water, clean air, and medicines. Healthy communities help regulate our climate and pollinate our crops. They also provide us with beautiful landscapes and recreational areas. By studying and maintaining biodiversity, we can help keep our planet healthy.

Brain Stretch

Sometimes areas become what is called a critical habitat. This happens when a species is threatened, or is near extinction, and needs protection. Laws to prevent killing, removing, or bothering of the species protect the critical habitat. This effort helps the species survive and thrive.

Create a poster about a critical habitat near your community. Make sure to include information on what caused this area to become a critical habitat. Describe what is being done to help this area recover.

"Biodiversity"—Think About It!

1. In what way is the classification of organisms the same as the classification of habitats?

2. The largest group of habitats is biomes. There are many types of biomes. Examples include deserts, forests, grasslands, tundra, and oceans. Choose a biome and create a brochure. Make sure your brochure has the following information on the biome: worldwide locations, climate, plants and animals, an example of a food chain, and interesting facts.

3. One type of forest is the temperate deciduous forest. Most trees in these forests lose their leaves in winter. These forests experience four seasons, with cold winters and warm summers. Deciduous forests receive precipitation all year and have fertile soil. Think about what you know about forests like this. Do research to find out more. On a separate piece of paper, draw then label plants and animals you might find in a temperate deciduous forest. Include some non-living things in your drawing.

4. How is the community you live in similar to a habitat community?

5. What do you think is the most important benefit humans get from biodiversity? Why?

Species Interactions

All organisms in a community have specific roles to play. Each species interacts with one or more other species. Most interactions involve competition for resources. Resources are things an organism needs to survive. These include food, water, air, sunlight, and shelter.

In a healthy community, there is a balance of organisms so each one gets what it needs. An example is the food pyramid. There are more species and individuals at the bottom of the pyramid. There are fewer and fewer as you move up the pyramid. When a community works the way it should, there is a balance in the number of species at all levels.

example of a food pyramid

Symbiosis

Some organisms have a special relationship with other organisms. Symbiosis is a close relationship between two or more organisms. At least one organism receives a benefit from this relationship. There are three categories of symbiosis.

- **Mutualism**—Both organisms benefit from the relationship. One example is between a zebra and a bird called an oxpecker. The oxpecker eats ticks and other parasites that live on the zebra's skin. The oxpecker gets food, and the zebra benefits from having the pests removed.

- **Commensalism**—One organism benefits from the relationship and the other is not affected. One example is the remora. This fish has an adhesive disk on its head. The remora uses this to stick to a larger animal such as a shark. When the shark is eating, scraps of food float away from the shark's mouth. The remora eats the scraps of food. The shark is not affected by the presence of the fish.

- **Parasitism**—One organism benefits from the relationship and the other is harmed in the process. One example is the flea. Fleas live on a host, such as a dog or cat. They bite their host's skin and suck their blood. The fleas get food and a warm home. But the host gets bitten repeatedly and is very itchy and uncomfortable.

"Species Interactions"—Think About It!

1. List these organisms in the order they would appear on a food pyramid, from bottom to top: mouse, corn, hawk, snake. Why would they be in this order?

____

____

____

2. Read the following descriptions. Tell whether each gives an example of mutualism, commensalism, or parasitism. Give reasons to support your answer.

   a) Burdock is a weed. The seed heads of the weed are burrs with hooked tips. These tips catch on cows, deer, or even people as they pass by. The burrs are dropped or brushed off in different places.

   ____

   ____

   b) A certain type of bacteria lives in human intestines. This bacteria eats food that humans cannot digest, and partially digests the food. Then the human finishes digesting the food.

   ____

   ____

   c) The deer tick attaches itself to an animal and feeds on the animal's blood.

   ____

   ____

3. Invasive species are organisms that are not naturally found in a community. They are usually brought in by people, sometimes for a reason and sometimes by accident. In 1998, zebra mussels were accidentally introduced into Lake St. Clair. They quickly spread throughout the Great Lakes and into many inland lakes, rivers, and canals. They have nearly eliminated the native clam population in the ecosystem. What effect can an invasive species have on a habitat community? Why?

____

____

____

____

Medicine from Plants

For thousands of years, people have relied on plants for food, building materials, and much more. One other very important way that plants help humans is by keeping them healthy.

Chemical Makers

Plants are able to make many chemicals that help them make food and grow. These chemical substances can also defend a plant again attacks from insects, fungi, and hungry animals. Scientists have been able to identify about 12,000 of these chemicals, but experts estimate that this is only about 10% of the total!

More than 120 of the chemical compounds used in modern medicine come from plants. People have known about the healing properties of plants' roots, leaves, flowers, bark, and berries since before written records were kept.

Bark and Leaves

The bark of the white willow contains a medicine commonly known as aspirin. People have used it for pain relief for more than 2,000 years. Another important medicine, digitalis, comes from the foxglove plant. This chemical has been used since the 1500s to treat heart disease.

Malaria is an often-fatal disease that is carried by mosquitoes. It kills thousands of people every year. The bark of the fever tree contains quinine, which is used to prevent and treat malaria. Another tropical plant, the aloe, has thick, fleshy leaves. The juice in these leaves contains alonin, a chemical that is used in medicine to cool burns, including sunburns.

aloe plant

More Help from Plants

Toothpick weed, or khella, is an herb from the area around the Mediterranean Sea. A chemical in this plant improves blood flow to the heart and helps the lungs work better. Scientists have used this plant to develop medicines to treat asthma and heart problems.

The Madagascar periwinkle has a small, bright-pink flower. This plant may alter the human immune system and is the source of a medicine used to treat diabetes and certain cancers. Meadow saffron also has a pinkish flower. But it is the bulb of this plant that has been used to treat rheumatism (painfully stiff arms, legs, and back) and gout (painful joints).

The rubber tree does not provide us with medicine, but with rubber to make such items as rubber gloves and waterproof sheeting that are important parts of health care and medicine.

continued next page

Plants in Danger

As the plants in habitats around the world are being destroyed, thousands of possibly life-saving medicines are disappearing. Scientists believe that plants, especially those that grow in rainforests, may contain cures for some of the world's deadliest diseases.

"Medicine from Plants"—Think About It!

1. Match the plant to the drug it contains:

   a) white willow tree   i)   quinine

   b) foxglove   ii) alonin

   c) fever tree   iii) aspirin

   d) aloe   iv) digitalis

2. How is the rubber tree different from the other plants mentioned in this article?

3. What are four ways that people have used plants? What are five plant parts people use?

4. People rely on plants. What does *rely* mean?

5. Why do people need to protect plants and where they live?

Adaptations

Organisms have characteristics that help them survive in their community. These adaptations can be physical structures or behaviors. Individuals with helpful traits are more likely to survive. They produce young with the same traits. Adaptations create biodiversity after many generations.

Structures

Physical features can help an organism survive. The beaks and feet of birds are good examples:

- short strong hooked beaks for eating animals
- long slender beaks dig in mud for food
- webbed feet for swimming
- a long back toe to perch on branches

Structural adaptations can also be inside an animal. For example, a penguin's heart beats 60 to 100 times per minute. When the penguin dives, its heart rate drops to 20 beats per minute. That helps the penguin use less oxygen.

Behaviors

The things organisms do are called behaviors. They can help them find food or survive harsh weather. Hibernating and migrating are two behavioral adaptations. Hunting is another behavior.

a change in color is a type of adaptation

Yummy fish swim into the shade made by a snowy egret's wings. Nice catch!

Brain Stretch

Write about why adaptations are important for an animal's survival. Use information from the text and your own ideas.

"Adaptations"—Think About It!

1. Choose two wild organisms—one plant and one animal. These organisms must live in your community habitat or another habitat that you know well. For each organism, describe one adaptation that helps the organism survive.

____

____

2. Read the descriptions below. For each, tell how the adaptation helps the organism survive.

a) The American alligator digs a den in the mud in very hot weather.

____

____

b) A beaver can close its lips behind its front teeth.

____

____

c) The eyes of a hippopotamus are on top of its head.

____

____

3. Many organisms live in habitats that make survival difficult. These habitats include deserts, the Arctic, or the ocean floor. Design an imaginary organism that could survive in one of these habitats. Choose a habitat, then draw and label a picture of your organism below. Make sure your organism has adaptations that would help the organism survive. On another piece of paper, write a short paragraph to explain how the adaptations help the organism.

How Biodiversity Benefits Humans

We get many things from other organisms. We get wood to build homes and get foods such as corn. Having many types of organisms gives us many resources.

Medicine

Humans have used plants as medicine throughout history. In ancient India, ginger was used for many things, including healing wounds and for stomachaches. The Gitxan peoples of British Columbia had many uses for a plant called Devil's club. The inner bark was used to heal wounds.

Plants are the starting point for many of the medicines today. The bark of the willow tree helps stop pain. An antibiotic comes from mold. The Pacific yew tree is the source of a cancer drug.

Clothes

Some cloth comes from plants. Flax turns into linen and cotton comes from cotton plants. Other fabrics come from animals. Silkworms make cocoons that we turn into silk. Wool comes from sheep, and leather comes from cows.

What Happens When There Is Less Diversity?

Less diversity can have a bad result. If there is only one type of corn, for example, bad weather could mean no corn grows. A single type of disease or pest could destroy the whole crop. But if there are many types of corn, some types could survive.

Growing only one type of plant takes out of the soil all the nutrients that plant needs. The soil then needs a lot of chemical fertilizer to grow more plants.

Some types of flowers will survive the pest that is eating the leaves.

Brain Stretch

Create a collage to show how humans benefit from biodiversity. Cut out pictures and words and paste them on a separate piece of paper.

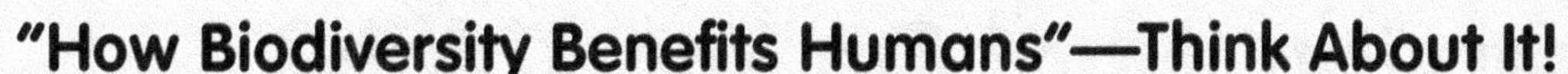

1. On a piece of paper, list products your family uses that come from other organisms. Use a graphic organizer such as a web to classify the products. Create your organizer below. Share your organizer with a classmate.

2. A field grows one type of sunflower very well. Why might the farmer plant only that sunflower?

____

____

____

____

3. One type of grass does not grow well in dry ground. Another type does not grow well in wet ground. Why might growing both grasses together make a healthy lawn?

____

____

____

____

Biodiversity: What Do You Think?

Think about the biodiversity in your city or community. What could be done to increase the biodiversity? You could plant a tree in your own backyard. Or an empty lot could be turned into a community garden. Talk about ideas with a classmate. Use your ideas to answer the questions below.

Think About It!

1. What could my family do? ____

____

____

____

____

2. What could our school do? ____

____

____

____

____

3. What could groups of people do? ____

____

____

____

____

4. What could the local government do? _______________________________________

____

____

____

____

Biodiversity Crossword Puzzle

Complete the crossword puzzle using words you have learned. On another piece of paper, use each word in a sentence that shows the word's meaning.

Across

2. class of animals with a spinal cord

7. animals without a backbone

10. an adaptation that is not a structure

Down

1. any living thing

3. characteristics of organisms that help them survive

4. things that move, reproduce, and grow are

5. the smallest part of an organism

6. different types of animals or plants together create this

8. the largest classification of organisms

9. a non-living thing that is all around you

All About Air

Air is all around you. You cannot live without air. Air makes flight possible, too. Planes and rockets, birds and bumblebees—every type of flying thing uses air.

Some Properties of Air

Unless the air around you is heavily polluted, you cannot see, taste, or smell the air. If you think you cannot feel air, take a deep breath. You can feel air rushing into your lungs.

Air also has mass or weight. A balloon weighs more after you fill the balloon with air. You experience the pressure air exerts on every surface. Closer to the ground, more air is pushing down on top on you and Earth's gravity pulls more. The higher up you go, the less air pressure there is. Air becomes thinner and more spread out.

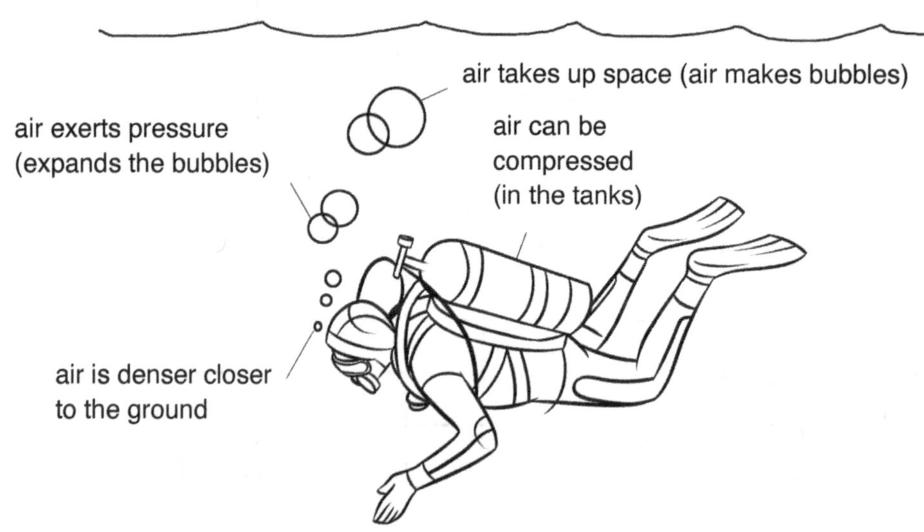

When it comes to flying, pressure is probably the most important property of air. Air pushes on every surface. Try this: Hold two pieces of paper out in front of you, about 3 in (8 cm) apart. Now blow between them. Did you expect the sheets to fly apart? They move closer together because the force of air on either side of the paper is unbalanced. The air moves quickly between the two papers. The moving air exerts less pressure than the air pressing on the outsides of the papers.

Aerodynamics means the motion of air and how air affects everything moving through it. People who design flying things have to know all about aerodynamics. This helps them build aircraft that fly efficiently and safely through the air.

"All About Air"—Think About It!

1. On another piece of paper, list all the things you know about air. For example, can air move? Can air move other things? Does air have a temperature? Can air rise or fall? Can air hold moisture? Write down how you know these things.

2. An experiment is shown in the diagrams below. The bottle contains only air. Diagram B shows what happened after the bottle was placed in hot water.

Heated air expands

a) How does the hot water affect the temperature of the air in the bottle?

____

____

b) When the bottle is placed in hot water, the balloon expands. What two things happened to the air in the bottle? How do you know?

____

____

c) Based on this experiment, what property of air could be added to the article "All About Air"?

____

____

d) If the bottle in diagram B is placed back in the cool water, what will happen to the balloon? Explain why.

____

____

Taking Flight

Find out about the four forces of flight: lift, weight, drag, and thrust.

Just a Little Lift

Lift helps an airplane overcome its weight. Lift also helps the plane rise into the air, and stay up in the air. Many parts of a plane work together to create lift. Most lift is generated by the wings.

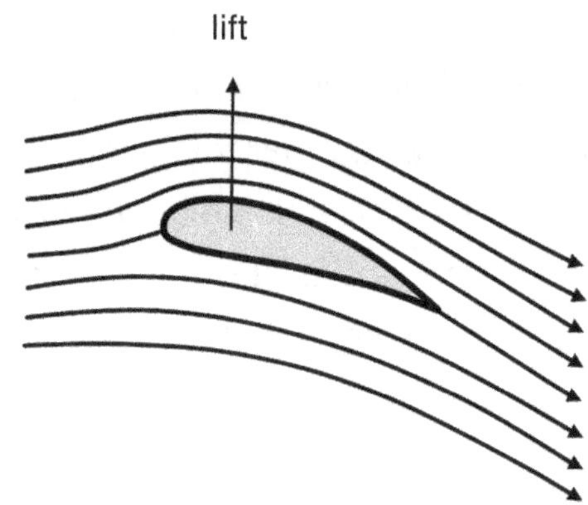

Look at a bird's wing when it is flying. You will see that it curves so that the top side is longer than the bottom. Planes create lift in the same way.

Air moving over the curved wing top goes farther than air going under the wing. The air also moves faster. Air that is moving more quickly exerts less pressure. So the air below the wing pushes up harder than the air above the wing pushes down. That lifts the plane into the air.

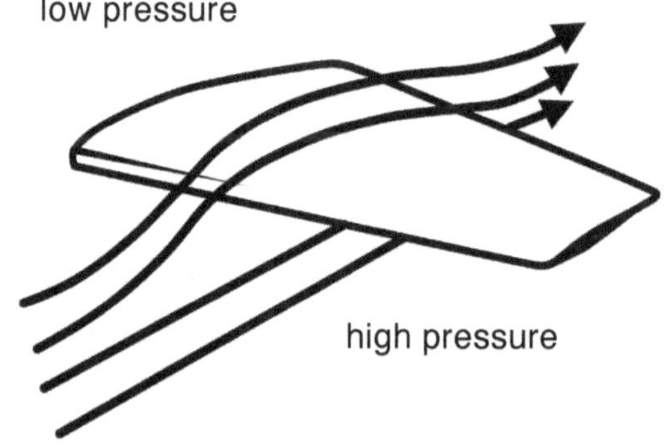

What a Drag!

When a plane moves through the air, the plane has to overcome drag. Drag is a force similar to friction. Drag slows down objects moving through air. Every part of a plane generates drag, even the engines.

The more streamlined, or aerodynamic, the plane is, the less drag the plane creates. The less drag the plane creates, the faster and more easily the plane can move through the air.

Overcoming Gravity

Earth's gravitational force makes it difficult for a plane to fly. You measure the force of gravity (weight) whenever you step on a scale. Gravity is a force that keeps a plane on the ground. The weight of a plane has to be overcome before it can fly.

Give It Some Power

Thrust is the force that propels an aircraft through the air. Thrust is used to overcome the plane's weight and the drag of the air on the plane.

Birds create thrust by flapping their wings. In an aircraft, thrust is generated by the engines. Thrust makes lift possible.

"Taking Flight"—Think About It!

1. Think about how the four forces of flight are related. Use the words below to complete the sentences.

drag	**land**	**less**	**lift**
more	**takeoff**	**thrust**	**weight**

a) ______________________ ______________________ must be greater than weight for a plane to

______________________ .

b) Thrust must be ______________________ than ______________________
for a plane to take off.

c) Lift must be less than a plane's ______________________ for the plane to

______________________ .

d) ______________________ has to be ______________________
than the drag for a plane to land.

2. Identify the force in each example: drag, lift, weight, or thrust.

a) A bird stretches out its wings for takeoff: ______________________

b) Sinking into mud: ______________________

c) Pushing with your foot to make a skateboard go faster: ______________________

d) Using a parachute to fall through the air more slowly: ______________________

A Short History of Flight

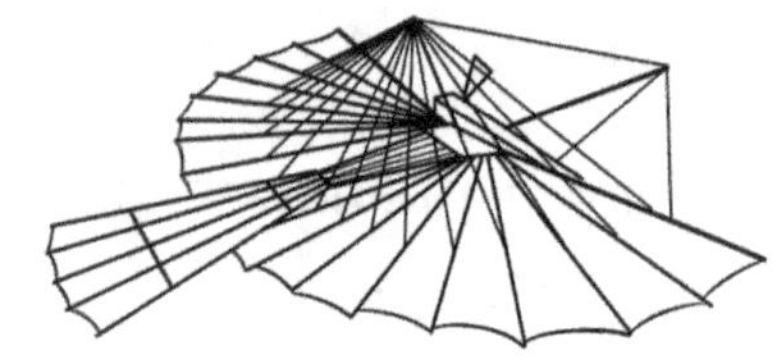

As far back as the year 1500, the inventor and painter Leonardo da Vinci drew airplane-like machines. He never built any of them, but he inspired other inventors.

Hot-Air Balloons

Since about 250, hot-air balloons were used as military signals in China. In 1783, brothers Joseph and Étienne Montgolfier had the idea of sending people up in a hot-air balloon. No one knew if there was air that far above Earth's surface. And, if there was air, was that air safe to breathe? Onlookers were amazed and shocked when it worked.

Bernoulli Principle

The hot-air balloon was a step forward in air travel, but the balloon could only drift in the wind. Inventors wanted a machine they could control. Serious inventors knew of the work of Daniel Bernoulli. In 1738, Bernoulli realized that the way air flows past a curved wing pushes or lifts it into the air.

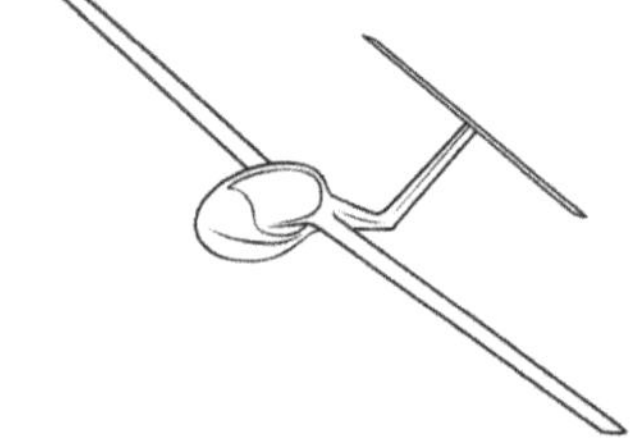

Using Bernoulli's principle, British experimenter Sir George Cayley designed several gliders. A glider depends on wind to move and stay aloft. A glider has no engine, but it can be steered. In 1849, Cayley launched a glider that carried a 10-year-old boy a short distance. That was the first time a glider had flown with a person onboard.

Cayley's work inspired Otto Lilienthal, a German engineer. By 1896, he had made about 2,000 glider flights. Lilienthal added an engine to power his glider, but it crashed, killing him.

Orville and Wilbur Wright

This tragedy frightened off many aircraft builders, but not American inventors Orville and Wilbur Wright. They were determined to add power to their gliders. In 1903, the Wright brothers became the first people to fly in a controlled and powered aircraft.

Better fighter aircraft were needed during World War II. In the early 1940s, airplanes became jet propelled. Today they are used to fly people for business or pleasure. They are also used to deliver goods around the world.

"A Short History of Flight"—Think About It!

1. Complete the timeline below to summarize information from "A Short History of Flight."
(Use bullets to list accomplishments.)

When	Who	Accomplishment

2. What do you think flight will be like 50 years from now? List your predictions on another piece of paper.

Flying Through the Sky

A car zooming along a road can move in just two different ways. A car can drive to the left or right and it can move up and down a hill. A plane can also tilt and twirl. Pilots use hinged flaps to change the shape of the plane in the air. This changes the aerodynamics and moves the plane.

The pilot can tilt the plane's nose up or down by tilting horizontal strips on the tail up or down.

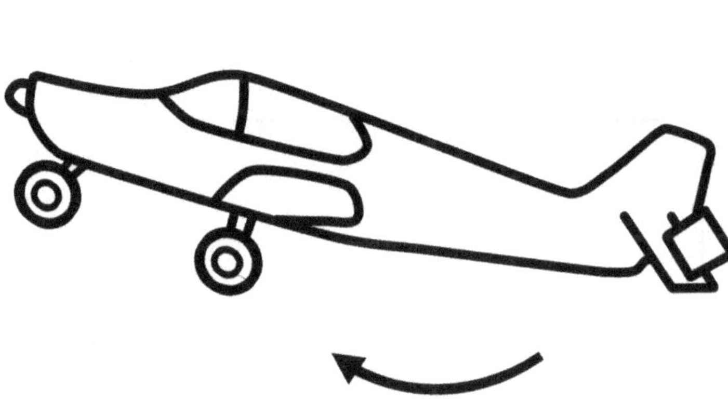

Flaps on the wings tilt up and down to roll the plane.

A hinged rudder on the vertical tail makes the plane turn left or right.

1. How does tilting a flap change the drag on a wing?

____

____

____

____

2. To go faster, should the flaps be flat or tilted? Explain why.

____

____

____

____

3. When a plane rolls, wind pushes up on one wing and down on the other wing. How does the pilot create these forces?

____

____

____

____

4. How could a bird change the tilt of its wings to slow down?

____

____

____

____

5. What force does the engine create?

____

____

____

____

Experiment: Build an Aircraft

Materials such as
- Paper or plastic bags
- Pipe cleaners, straws, craft sticks
- Glue, tape, paper clips
- Measuring tape, timer

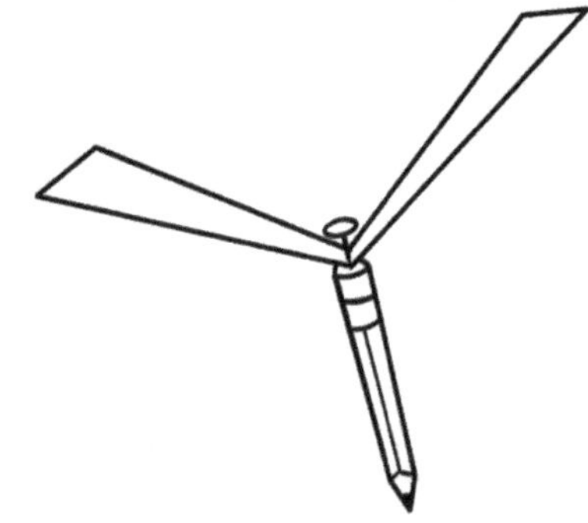

What You Do

1. Decide what type of aircraft you will build. For example, you might build an airplane, a spinner, or a glider.
2. Draw a plan and list the materials you need.
3. Decide how you will test the aircraft. Will you test the steering, time in the air, distance traveled, or all three?
4. Build the aircraft and conduct flight tests.
5. Record your findings.

Test	Flight Time	Distance Traveled	Steering
1			
2			
3			

Think About It!

1. Did your aircraft fly the way you thought it would? Explain.

____

____

2. What changes could make your aircraft fly better? Explain why.

____

____

____

Aircraft with Motors

Amphibious Aircraft

Aircraft that can land and take off either on land or water are amphibious. Some have skis so they can also land on snow or ice. Amphibious aircraft are especially useful in remote areas where they can land on runways, lakes, or rivers.

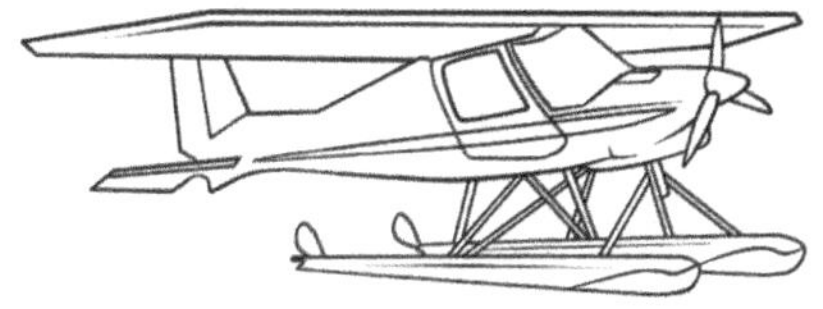

Helicopters

Helicopters get lift and thrust from the propellers—a rotor on the top. This rotor allows helicopters to take off and land vertically. It also lets the helicopter hover, and fly forward, backward, and sideways. Helicopters are often used in areas where there is no room for an airplane runway.

Stealth Planes

Stealth aircraft are military aircraft. These planes use advanced technology to avoid being detected by radar. Stealth planes have features that interfere with radar. These features make the plane difficult to see, hear, or detect with hi-tech equipment. However, these aircraft can be detected when they use their weapons. Stealth planes can have human pilots. They can also be flown by remote control.

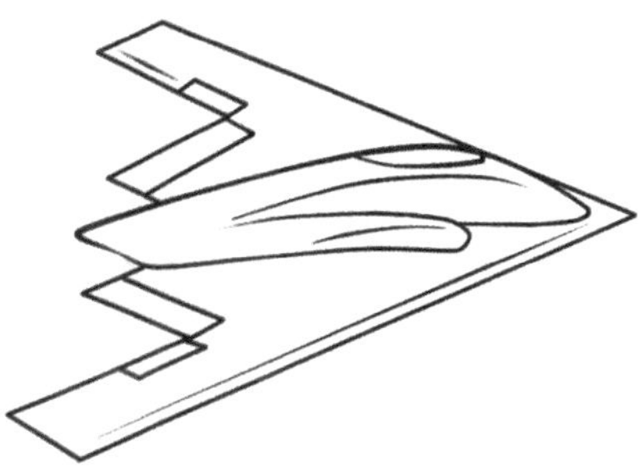

Think About It!

1. People are searching for a hiker lost in the wilderness. Give three reasons why a helicopter would be better to search with than an airplane.

____

____

____

____

____

Aircraft Without Motors

Some aircraft do not need a motor.

Hot-Air Balloons

To take a ride in a hot-air balloon, you climb into the basket that hangs from the huge balloon. In the basket is a source of heat that warms the air in the balloon. This warm air makes the balloon rise. Hot-air balloons are used for recreation. They are also used to send weather recording devices high into the sky.

Kites

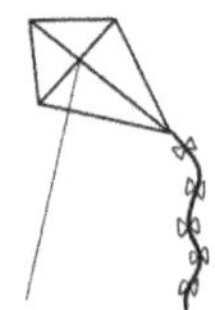

Kites are some of the oldest flying objects. Kites have been used as signals. They have also been used to take pictures from high in the sky, and to lift scientific instruments. Today, kites are mostly used for fun. Maybe you flew a kite at the park. Some people use very large kites to pull them across the water or snow.

Gliders

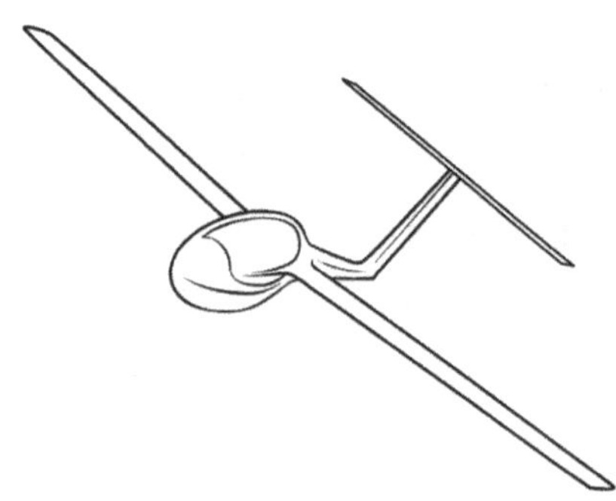

Because they have no engines, gliders depend on wind and air currents to keep them in the sky. Many gliders need a plane to get them up in the air. They are only designed to descend. Gliders are mostly used for sports such as gliding and hang gliding. They are also used for flight research. Paper airplanes that you make are actually gliders.

Think About It!

1. Hot-air balloons use very little fuel compared to other aircraft. What are two disadvantages of hot-air balloons?

____

____

2. In what ways is a kite similar to a glider?

____

____

Space Flight

In 1957, Russian engineers launched the first artificial satellite into space. A satellite is an object that orbits a planet or the Sun. This amazing event happened just 54 years after the Wright brothers' first flight.

One of the toughest obstacles to space travel is overcoming Earth's gravity. Doing this takes rocket power— extremely strong thrust from a rocket engine. These engines push rockets up by ejecting exhaust downward very quickly.

Sending people beyond the moon will be very difficult. How will they have enough oxygen, water, or food to survive the long trip out and back? People experience very little gravity in space. The human body has difficulty staying healthy in microgravity conditions.

Another obstacle to space travel is radiation. The Sun gives off many forms of radiation, including Xrays. This radiation penetrates spacecraft walls and astronauts' bodies. Earth's atmosphere helps protect us from this radiation. There is no protective atmosphere in space.

space shuttle

Brain Stretch

You have been hired to promote the importance of investigating space travel. On a separate piece of paper, draft a persuasive radio commercial. Use this checklist to help you. When you are finished, share your radio commercial with the class.

- ❑ My commercial is 15 to 30 seconds long.
- ❑ My commercial has a clear message about the benefits of space travel.
- ❑ I created the commercial to appeal to my target audience. (kids or adults)
- ❑ I practiced reading my commercial with expression.

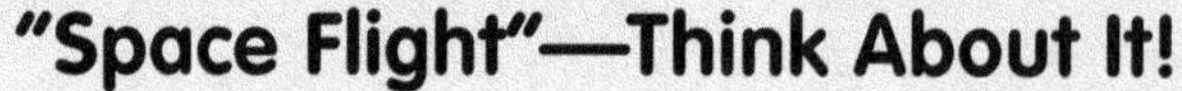

1. List the source of each force during a rocket launch.

a) thrust: ____

b) lift: ____

c) drag: ____

d) gravity: ____

2. What are some problems people will have to overcome for long-term space travel?

____

____

____

____

3. Satellites take photos from space and transmit signals for radio and phones. What disadvantages do satellites have?

____

____

____

____

____

____

____

____

communications satellite

Animal Fliers

You have learned a lot about machines that fly. Many animals can fly, too.
Some have wings. Some have feathers. Others stretch skin into a wing shape.

Insects

Insects are amazing fliers because they can turn their wings. That lets them hover in the air or even fly backwards. Dragonflies have two sets of wings that help them quickly stop and change direction mid-flight.

Bats

When you look at a bat's wing, you may see long bony fingers with a thin skin or membrane stretched between them. Bats flap their spread-out fingers to fly.

bat

Birds

Birds flap their wings to propel them through the air. They change the shape and angle of their wings to take off, steer, and land. Some birds are excellent gliders and barely flap their wings.

eagle

Think About It!

1. Animals that fly have very light skeletons. An animal of similar size that does not fly is much heavier. How does a light skeleton help a flying animal?

____

____

____

____

2. List a reason why each of the following are able to fly:

Insects: ____

Bats: ____

Birds: ____

Furred and Finned Gliders

Squirrels

A flying squirrel can not really fly, but it is an excellent glider. It can coast farther than the length of three hockey rinks! First, a flying squirrel opens up a flap of furry skin that stretches from each wrist to each ankle. Then it glides with its body spread out. Its tail is puffed out so it works like a parachute.

flying squirrel

Reptiles

When a flying lizard unfurls its wings, it is easy to see the ribs that support the wings. The ribs and attached membrane spread out to form a semicircle on each side of the lizard's body. When these wings are not in use, they fold back against the animal's sides.

flying lizard

Fish

Flying fish cover long distances by making a series of glides through the air. At the end of each glide, a flying fish dips its tail into the water. This action produces new forward thrust. Flying squid propel themselves out of the water by expelling water. These creatures usually glide through the air only when they need to escape predators.

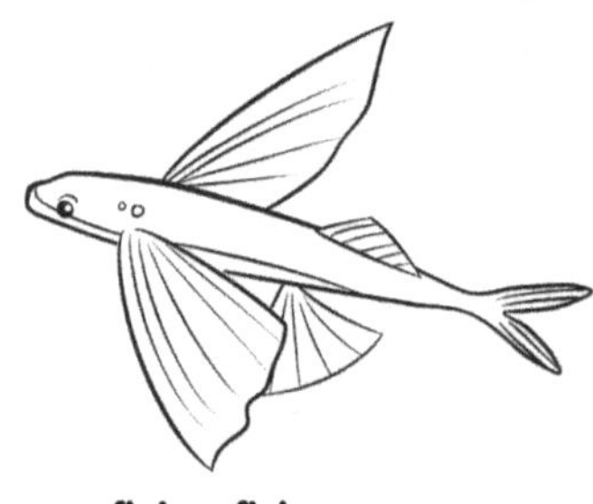

flying fish

Other Fliers

It is not only animals that use wings and air currents to get around. Dandelion seeds use their fluff like a parachute to float to new environments. Maple keys spin through the air like a helicopter or fall slowly. This helps them move away from the tree where they were produced.

Think About It!

1. Imagine a toy that would fly like an animal. What design features should it have? List two things.

____

____

____

____

Airplanes

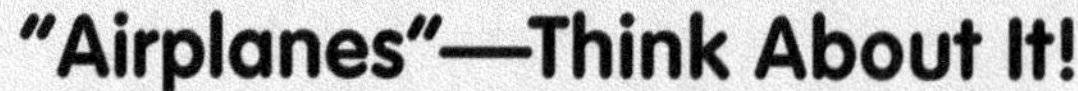

"Airplanes"—Think About It!

1. Look at the picture on the previous page. In the chart, note the pros and cons of airplane travel. (Use bullet points.) Include any additional ideas you have.

Pros	Cons

2. How might these groups feel about airplane travel? Why?

a) People who work in the aircraft industry or in airports: _______________________________

____

____

b) People who live very close to an airport: _______________________________________

____

____

c) People who must travel to see doctors: _______________________________________

____

____

Flight Quiz

See how many of these questions you can answer before you look back at the articles in this unit or other resources.

1. What are the four forces of flight?

____

____

____

____

2. What property of air is illustrated by blowing up a balloon?

____

3. All the air in one container can be forced into a smaller container. What property of air does this show?

____

4. An inflated balloon weighs slightly more than it does when it is not inflated. What property of air does this show?

____

continued next page ☞

5. a) Air flows past a curved wing. Why does the air moving under the wing exert more
   pressure than the air moving over the wing?

____

____

____

____

   b) Air pushes up on the wings. The pressure above the wing is not as strong as the
   pressure under the wing. What force is this?

____

6. What effect does drag have on objects moving through the air?

____

____

____

____

7. What generates the thrust that helps a rocket take off?

____

8. Drag is a force to overcome. How is drag useful to control flight?

____

____

____

____

Amelia Earhart

Amelia Earhart was an American aviator who broke many flying records. Today, she is even more famous for vanishing… without a trace.

Up in the Air

This high flyer was born in 1897 in Kansas. When she finished high school, Amelia was not sure what she wanted to do. So she worked as a nurse and decided she would study medicine. But that all changed when she took her first ride in a plane. As soon as the plane was just a short way off the ground, Amelia knew that she had to learn to fly.

The Canary

When Amelia was back on the ground, she immediately began working hard to earn enough money to pay for flying lessons. Eventually, she bought her own plane. It was bright yellow, so she called it "The Canary." Amelia soon had her pilot's license and was ready to fly.

In 1928, Amelia was asked to take part in a flight across the Atlantic Ocean from the United States to Wales in Great Britain. Flying with a pilot and co-pilot, Amelia was the navigator. She was the first woman to be carried by plane across the Atlantic. She returned to the United States a hero, although she did not think she deserved all the attention she received. Instead, she became determined to fly across the ocean by herself.

Across the Atlantic

In 1932, Amelia took off from Harbour Grace, Newfoundland. It was not long before she ran into bad weather and thick clouds. Her windshield and wings were often covered with ice.

Amelia was aiming for Paris, but she had to cut her flight short and land in Northern Ireland. However, she became the first woman to pilot a plane solo across the Atlantic Ocean. Only one man, Charles Lindbergh, had successfully flown solo across the ocean before her.

Vanished!

Amelia was the most famous woman in the world, but she still was not satisfied. She wanted to be the first woman to fly all around the world. So, in June 1937, she and her navigator Fred Noonan took off from Miami, Florida.

Planes could not fly as far back then, so they had to make a number of stops. First, the pair flew to Puerto Rico, then east to Africa. They flew to Pakistan, then India, and soon were in New Guinea in the south Pacific Ocean.

continued next page 

On July 2, Amelia and Fred took off to fly to Howland Island in the Pacific Ocean. They were never seen again. No trace has ever been found of this brave pilot or her plane, and her final flight remains a mystery.

"Amelia Earhart"—Think About It!

1. What is the main idea of this article?

2. What accomplishments made Amelia the most famous woman in the world?

3. Do you like to fly? Give three reasons why or why not.

4. Amelia did not think she deserved all the attention she received. What does this mean and what does it tell you about her personality?

5. What do you think happened to Amelia? Give three reasons for your conclusion.

6. On a separate piece of paper, write a news article detailing Amelia Earhart's accomplishments and her disappearance. Use information from the text and other research tools for your article.

Article Checklist

Content

☐ An attention-grabbing headline names the article.

☐ The byline shows my name as the author.

☐ The beginning gives the most important facts.

☐ The middle gives supporting details about the main idea.

☐ The ending gives the reader an idea to remember.

Grammar and Style

☐ I used my neatest printing and included a clear headline.

☐ I included a colorful picture to support my article.

☐ I used descriptive language.

☐ I checked the spelling.

☐ I checked the punctuation.

Using Electricity

Electricity is a form of energy that we use in many ways every day. You probably use electricity much more than you realize. Look at the pictures. Think about which things use electricity.

Electricity provides the energy that makes devices work. Some devices get electricity from batteries. Other devices get electricity from a wall outlet. You plug the device into the outlet and electricity travels into the device through the wire.

Where Does Electricity Come From?

Electricity is produced in a power plant by machines called generators. The generators are powered by a fuel such as coal or natural gas. Generators can also be powered by wind or water.

The electricity produced by the power plant travels over wires called transmission lines. Some of these transmission lines are attached to tall metal towers, and others are attached to poles along streets. In many places, electrical wires are buried underground. The wires provide electricity to homes, schools, factories, and other buildings.

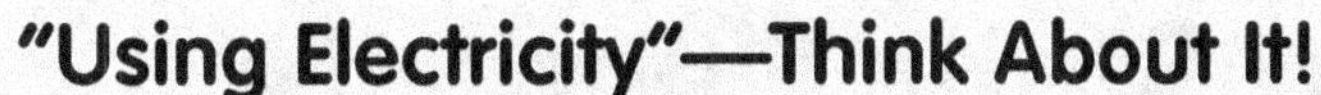

"Using Electricity"—Think About It!

1. How do people use electricity at home? Rank the examples, starting with number 1 for the item that you think uses the most electricity over a year.

2. Electricity is used indoors and outdoors. List at least three ways that electricity is used outdoors.

3. Many of the devices we use every day run on electricity from batteries. List at least four devices that use batteries. (Remember that any rechargeable device has a battery inside.)

4. Electricity in wall outlets is not available during a power blackout. Describe how life would be different for you and your family during a blackout.

Current and Static Electricity

Static Electricity

Pull a wool hat off and your hair tries to stand on end. Walk across a carpet and you may get a shock when you touch something. Why does this happen?

When objects rub, a charge builds up on the surface. The charge can be positive or negative, like the poles on a battery. You cannot see the charge on an object, but you might see what the charge does. The charge makes hairs stand up and balloons stick to walls. The charge can also make a stream of water bend toward the charge.

Because the charge stays in place for a while, we call this charge static electricity. When the charge moves from one object to another, you may see—and feel—the spark.

Current Electricity

Current electricity flows along a path called a circuit. A circuit connects the source of electricity to a load that does something useful. The source might be a power plant, or it might be a battery. A lightbulb is one type of load.

Think About It!

1. Circle the examples that use current electricity.

   shock from walking on carpet　　**flashlight**　　**lightning**

   power lines in a house　　**solar calculator**　　**light switch**

2. Items with the same charge push apart from each other. Items with opposite charges are attracted to each other. Do these items have the same charge or opposite?

   a) A balloon sticks to a wall. _______________________

   b) Hairs push away from each other so hard that they stand straight up. _______________________

3. When clothes come out of the dryer, some may stick together. We call this "static cling" because static electricity causes the clothing to cling. Explain what happens to make the clothes stick together.

   ____

   ____

Experiment: Electric Cereal

Try this experiment to see static electricity at work.

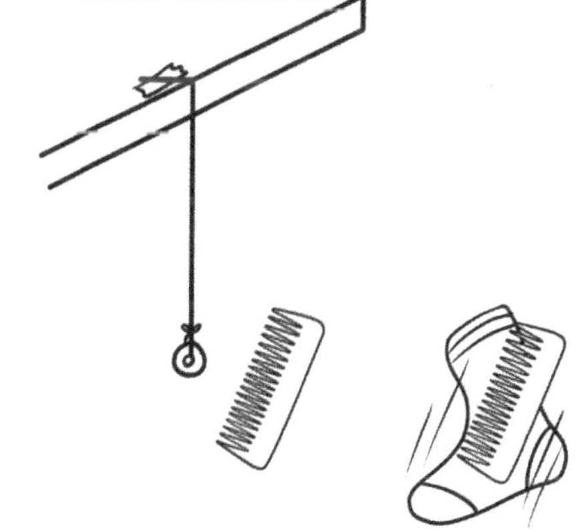

What You Need

- Hard plastic comb
- Liquid soap
- Dish towel or paper towel
- 12 in (30 cm) of thread
- Piece of dry O-shaped cereal
- Wool mitten or sock
- Table
- Tape
- Balloon (optional)

What You Do

1. Tie one end of the thread to a piece of cereal.
2. Tape the other end of the thread to the top of a table, so the cereal hangs in the air. The cereal should not be too close to anything.
3. Wash the comb with soap to make sure there is no oil on the comb. Carefully rinse away all of the soap. Dry the comb with the towel. (Make sure the comb is completely dry.)
4. Rub the comb quickly on the wool for several moments. Predict what will happen when you bring the comb close to the cereal.
5. a) *Slowly* bring the comb close to the cereal. Do not touch the comb to the cereal. At a certain point, the cereal should move. Record what happens.

   b) Hold the comb still until the cereal moves again. Note how the cereal moves this time.
6. Once again, slowly bring the comb closer to the cereal. See if you can make the comb touch the cereal. Record what happens.

Optional

7. If a balloon is available, blow the balloon up and tie off the end. Repeat steps 4 through 6, using the balloon instead of the comb. Note any differences in the results.

1. Record the results of your experiment in the chart below. Use drawings or words.

What I Did	What I Saw
Slowly moved the comb close to the cereal **(Step 5 a)**	
Held the comb still until the cereal moved again **(Step 5 b)**	
Tried to touch the comb to the cereal **(Step 6)**	

2. How does the comb become electrified?

____

____

3. Is this an example of static electricity or current electricity? Explain.

____

____

4. Did the comb and wool cause the effect you saw? Did the cereal cause the effect you saw? Describe a step you could add to test this.

____

____

Conductors and Insulators

Electricity flows through wires to make devices work. Electrical wires run through the walls in a house. Can electricity flow through all types of material? No. Some materials block the path of electricity.

A conductor is any material that electricity can flow through easily. Metals, water, and people all conduct electricity. Metal conducts electricity best.

An insulator is any material that electricity cannot flow through. An electric charge cannot move easily through rubber, plastic, glass, or wood.

Conductors and Insulators in Daily Life

Electrical cords on devices such as televisions and lamps are covered in plastic. Inside the plastic is a metal wire. These metal wires are often made of copper. Copper is a good conductor.

Electricity flows through the wire, but not through the plastic. That means you can touch the cord without getting a shock.

When electricians work, they protect themselves by wearing thick rubber gloves. The gloves prevent electricity from flowing into the worker.

Brain Stretch

A finger can operate a touch screen. A tiny amount of electric charge in the touch screen moves into the finger. This tells the device where the finger is pointing. Do you think you could use a touch screen while wearing gloves? Explain.

"Conductors and Insulators"—Think About It!

1. After a big storm, you notice that one of the power lines on the street has snapped. One end of the power line is lying in a large puddle. You notice that the power line has a thick rubber coating on the outside. Would getting close to the snapped power line be dangerous? Would getting close be dangerous even if you did not touch the power line? Explain why or why not.

____

____

____

2. Electricians often use tools that have rubber handles. Why is this a good idea?

____

____

____

3. Imagine that you found an old lamp. The lamp's cord is covered in cloth, not plastic. Some of the cloth is falling apart. In one place, you can see the wire inside the cord. Explain why this is dangerous.

____

____

4. Categorize the materials listed below using the T-chart. Add your own examples.

pencil
coin
plastic button
stove element
rubber boots
safety pin
wood table
magnet
glass
touch screen
earphone wire
tires

Conductors	Insulators

Using Water to Produce Electricity

Hydro means "water." Hydroelectric power plants use water to create electricity.

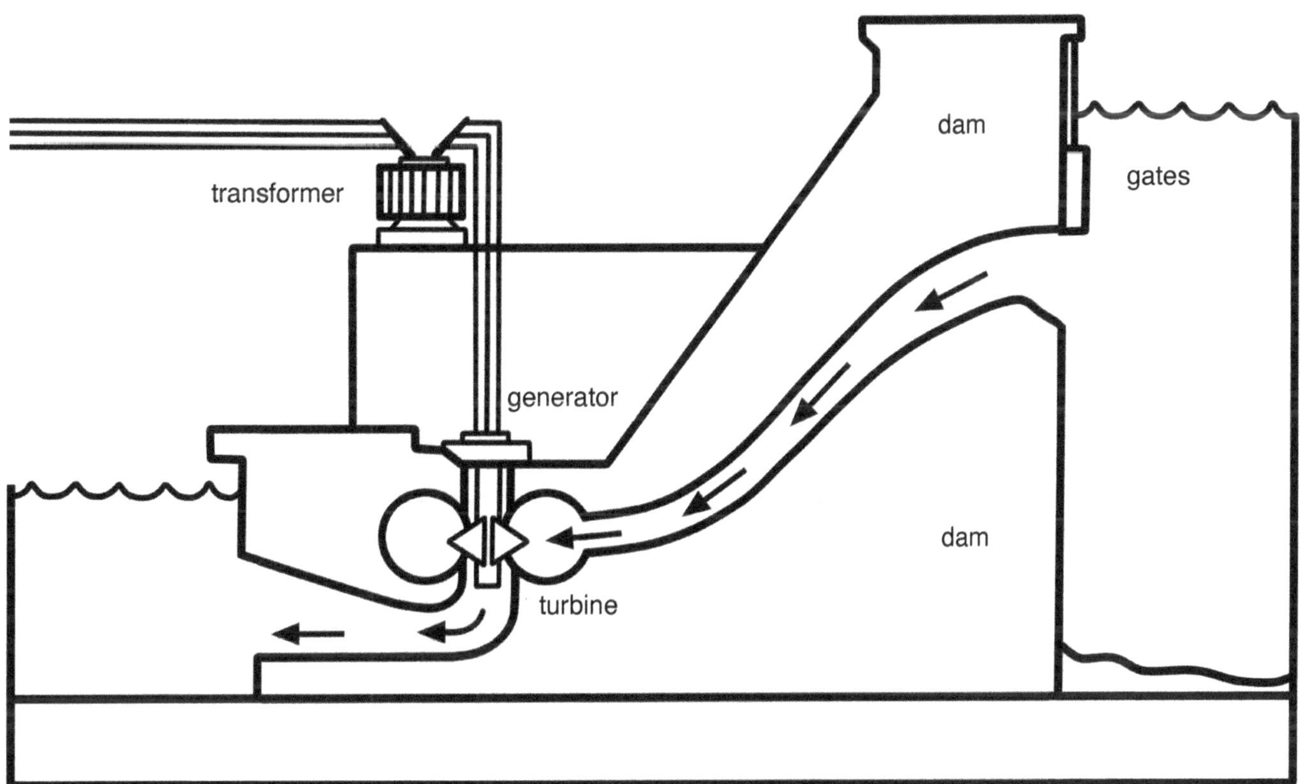

How It Works

1. A dam is built in a river. Water collects behind the dam, creating a lake or reservoir.

2. When the gates are open, water rushes down a pipe to the turbines.

3. The water turns the turbine blades, which turns the rod the blades are attached to.

4. The turbine makes the rod and magnets spin very quickly inside the generator. As the magnets spin, charge builds up in coils of copper wire, creating electricity.

5. The electricity travels along wires to the transformer. The transformer can help send electricity far away to where electrical power is needed.

"Using Water to Produce Electricity"—Think About It!

1. Explain how each group might feel about a hydroelectric dam being built.

a) People who live along the edge of the river where the lake will be created

b) People who enjoy boating and waterskiing

c) Unemployed workers who live near the building site

d) People who believe that an earthquake might happen where dam will be built

2. If you lived close to the site of the proposed dam, how would you feel about the dam? Explain why.

Using Wind to Produce Electricity

People have used wind power for centuries. Early windmills turned grinding stones that crushed grain into flour. Today we use windmills to create electricity.

How Wind Turbines Work

You can think of a wind turbine as the opposite of a fan. A fan uses electricity to make its blades turn, and the turning blades produce moving air. A wind turbine uses moving air (wind) to turn its blades. The movement of the blades produces electricity.

1. Wind turns the windmill's blades.

2. The blades turn the main shaft (rod) attached to them.

3. Gears in the gear box speed up the spinning motion. The second shaft then spins even faster. The faster the magnets spin, the more electricity is produced.

4. The turbine shaft and magnets spin very quickly inside the generator.

5. As the magnets spin, charge builds up in coils of copper wire. This creates electricity.

6. The electricity travels along wires to where it is needed.

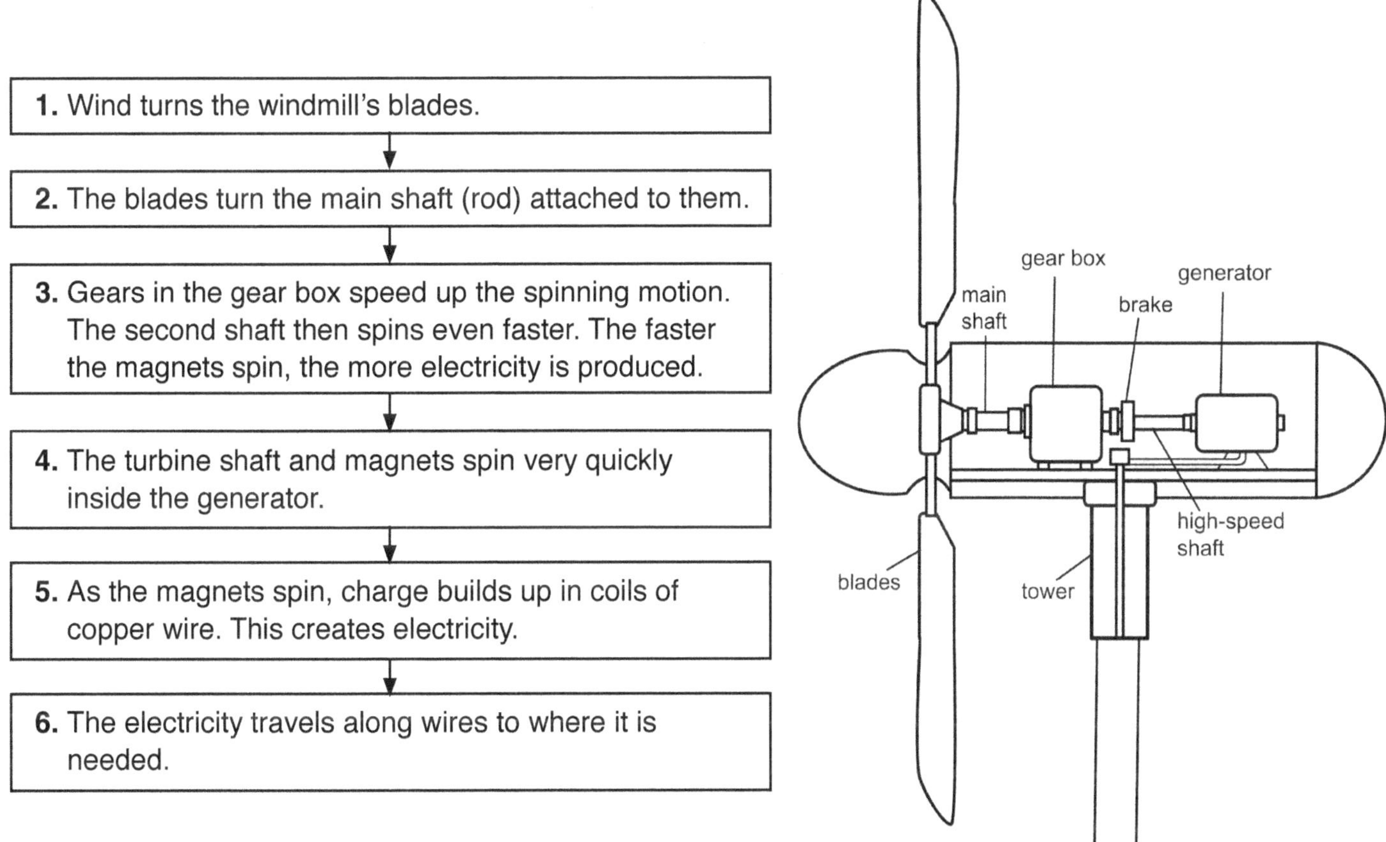

Wind Farms

A wind farm is a place that has a lot of wind turbines. The area must be flat and open, with a lot of wind. A wind farm can be built over water, such as a lake or ocean.

Advantages of Wind Turbines	Disadvantages of Wind Turbines
• create electricity • do not create pollution • many possible locations	• noisy • can be seen from quite far away • turning blades can kill or injure birds and bats

1. Why should wind turbine blades be very lightweight?

____

____

____

____

2. Wind turbines do not pollute the environment when they operate. But the metal, concrete, and other materials used to make them must be produced. The turbines must also be built and sent to the site. How can producing these materials affect the environment?

____

____

____

____

3. Review the information about hydroelectric power plants. In the chart below, list similarities and differences between a hydroelectric power plant and a wind turbine. (Use bullet points.)

Similarities	Differences

Transforming Energy

Energy exists in different forms. Electricity is one type of energy. Heat, light, and sound are also forms of energy. Motion is another form of energy.

You can change one form of energy into another. In fact, you do this every day. You turn motion into heat when you rub your hands together. A lightbulb turns electricity into light. A wall clock turns electrical energy into the motion of the hands.

Some devices give more forms of energy than we want. A blender makes motion (the blades turn), sound energy (noise), and heat (the motor warms up). Sound and heat energy do not help the blender accomplish the task of blending food.

A blender makes motion by turning the blades.

Think About It!

Each device below turns electrical energy into another form of energy. Check off the forms of energy that each device uses to do its job. Add more devices to the chart.

Device	Transforms electrical energy into			
	Heat	Light	Sound	Motion
a) Television				
b) Iron				
c) Electric can opener				
d)				
e)				
f)				

All About Electrical Circuits

What Is a Circuit?

A circuit is the path that electricity travels along. Here are the parts of a simple circuit:

Part	What It Does	Example
Power source	provides electricity	battery
Conductor	carries the electrical current	metal wire
Load	uses electricity to do something useful	motor

The purpose of a circuit is to provide electricity to the load. If there is a gap anywhere in the circuit, the load will not work. The electric current will not be able to flow through the load. The load in the diagram is a lightbulb. If there is a gap in the circuit, the lightbulb will not light.

In the simple circuit, the electric current flows from the battery. The current flows through the lightbulb, and back into the battery. The ends of the two wires are connected to the battery and to the lightbulb. There are no gaps in the circuit, so the circuit is complete.

If there is a gap in a circuit, the electric current will not be able to flow through the circuit.

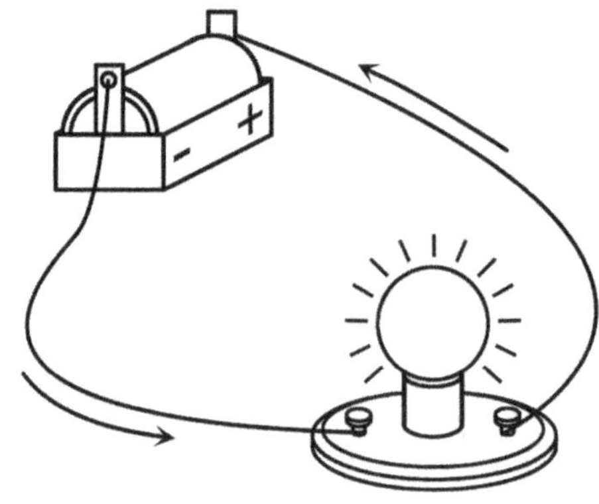

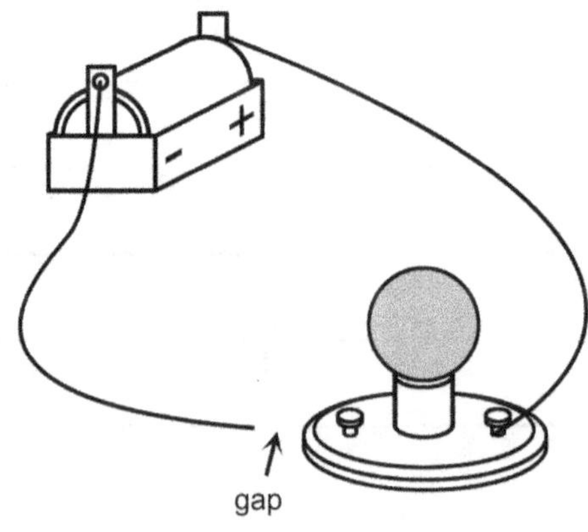

continued next page

What Is a Series Circuit?

A series circuit connects several loads.
There is only one path for the electric
current to flow along.

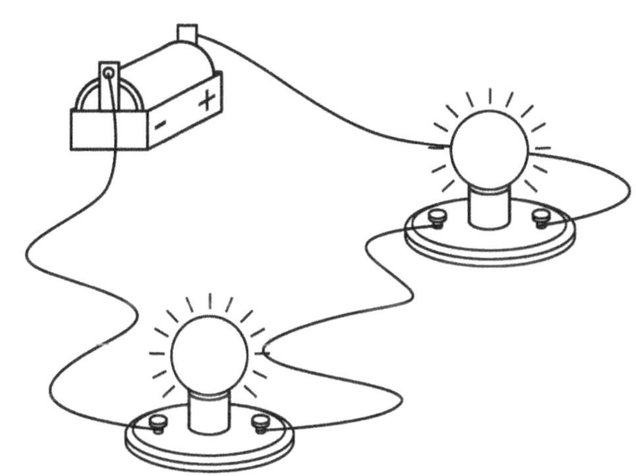

What Is a Parallel Circuit?

A parallel circuit provides more than one path for the electric current to flow on.
Use your finger to trace these paths on the diagram:

Path 1: A → B → E → F
Path 2: A → B → C → D → E → F

In a parallel circuit, the electric current flows through all the possible paths. This happens only if
each path is complete. In the circuit above, some of the current follows Path 1 and some follows
Path 2. Both lightbulbs light up.

1. Incandescent lightbulbs light up when electric current passes through a thin wire inside the bulb. We say the bulb is "burned out" when the wire has broken. In the circuit shown, lightbulb *A* is burned out.

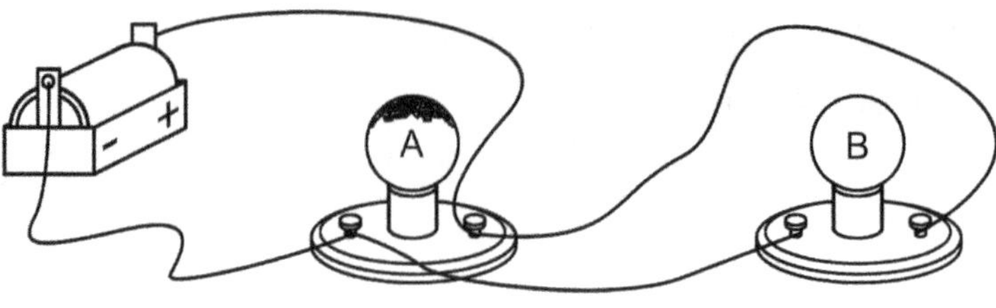

   a) Is this a series circuit or a parallel circuit? Explain your answer.

   ____

   ____

   b) Will lightbulb *B* light up? Explain why or why not.

   ____

   ____

2. When you use a switch to turn off a light, electric current no longer flows through the lightbulb. Use what you know about circuits to explain how a switch turns off a lamp.

   ____

   ____

   ____

3. A string of patio lights has a parallel circuit. What are two benefits of this type of circuit?

   ____

   ____

4. a) Look at the diagram below. Is the mystery material a conductor or an insulator? How do you know?

   ____

   ____

   b) What could the mystery material be made of? Name three possible materials.

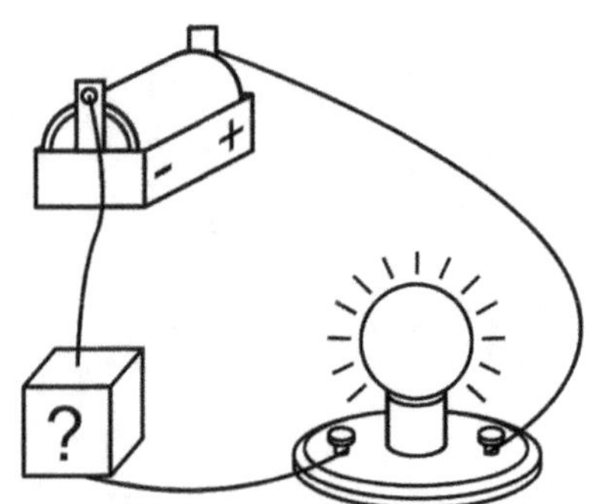

   ____

   ____

Life Without Electricity

If you could travel back in time, you would find that life was very different.

Cooking

The stove was heated by burning wood or coal. A lot of time was spent chopping wood to burn. The burnt wood or coal left ash behind. All that ash had to be cleaned out of the stove regularly.

Refrigeration

To keep food from spoiling, it was kept in an ice box. There were two doors on the ice box. The top door opened to a small compartment where a big block of ice was stored. The bottom door opened to a larger compartment. Foods such as milk and butter were stored there.

In a city, a truck regularly delivered ice for the ice box. People in the countryside often cut blocks of ice from a frozen lake in winter. By covering the blocks with thick layers of hay or grass, they could make the ice last through most of the summer—if they were lucky.

continued next page

Lighting

Lamps that burned a fuel called kerosene were common. These gave off dirty smoke. You had to clean the lamps often, and add more kerosene.

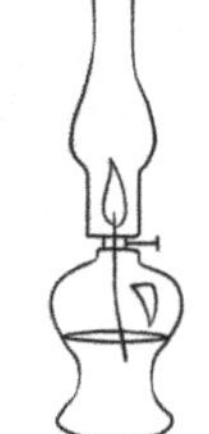

Warm Baths

The bath was moved into the kitchen to be close to the stove. Hot water was heated on the stove. Filling the tub took time, and heating water used up fuel. An entire family often took turns using the same bath water.

Laundry

Clothes were washed in soapy water and rubbed against a washboard to get them clean. The clothes were then rinsed in clean water. People did not do laundry on a rainy day because clothing had to hang outside to dry.

Ironing the wrinkles out of clothes was not much fun. The iron was made of solid iron. It was very heavy. The iron was heated on the stove. A rag or potholder was used on the very hot handle. The iron had to be reheated frequently on the stove.

Communication

There were no telephones or Internet. Messages were delivered by a person walking or riding a horse. Letters took days and sometimes weeks to reach their destination.

"Life Without Electricity"—Think About It!

Complete the chart below to show how we use electricity in daily life today. Then suggest how you might use less electricity for each task.

Task	How this task is done today	How I can save electricity
a) Cooking		
b) Refrigeration and freezing		
c) Lighting		
d) Warm baths		
e) Laundry		
f) Communication		

Electricity Crossword

Complete the crossword puzzle to review your knowledge of electricity.

Down

1. This type of electricity flows along a path

2. A material often used as an insulator on power cords

3. Type of material in which electricity flows easily

5. The part of a circuit that uses electricity to do something useful

6. Friction causes this to build up

8. You can see through this type of insulator

9. A small and portable power source

Across

2. Energy, such as electricity, is produced in this type of plant

4. Any material that stops the flow of electricity

7. The type of electricity caused by friction

8. The part of a hydroelectric power plant or wind turbine that produces electricity

10. This type of circuit has more than one path that electricity can flow along

11. In a series circuit with four lightbulbs, this is the number of bulbs that will light up when one bulb has burned out

Create an Electricity Game

What You Need

- Scissors
- Thumbtack
- Card stock
- Note paper
- Coloring materials
- Large paper clip

What You Do

Build a Spinner

1. Cut a large circle from the card stock. Divide the circle into 6 to 9 slices.
2. Decide on an electricity-related category for each slice of the spinner. Make one category a question.

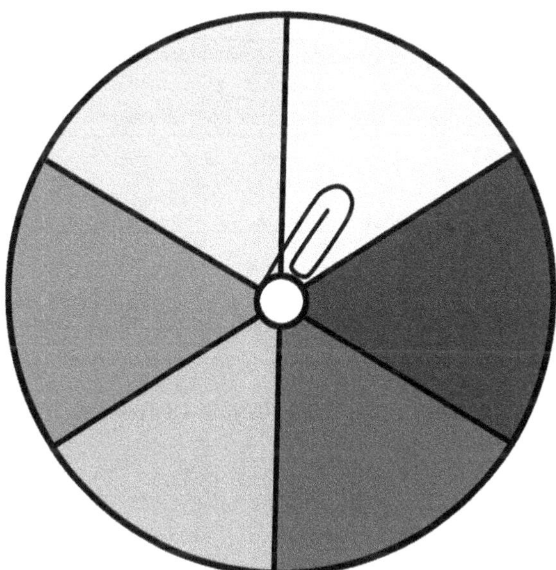

3. Use the thumbtack to secure the paper clip in the center of the spinner.

continued next page 

Write Question Cards

1. Divide sheets of notepaper into at least 20 question cards.

2. Look through your notes to write questions about the following:

- electricity
- circuits
- power generation
- safety
- energy conservation

Include the following types of questions:
- true or false
- multiple choice
- explain something
- draw a picture

3. Write questions on the cards. Include the answers and points.

Write the Rules

1. How many people can play? _______________________________

2. Who keeps score? _______________________________

3. What is the penalty for a wrong answer? _______________________________

____

4. When does the game end? It might be timed, last a certain number of turns, or have a winning score.

____

Test your game with some classmates. After playing, adjust the rules and add questions to make the game better.

Our Sun Is a Star

Earth circles around the Sun. The Sun is a star and we could not live without it. The Sun is a ball of burning gas that gives us light and heat. The light makes plants grow, which provides us with food and with oxygen to breathe. The Sun's heat gives us rain by warming oceans and lakes. When that happens, some of the water evaporates into water vapor, which floats into the sky. When the water vapor rises high enough, it hits cooler air and condenses, and eventually falls as rain.

How big is the Sun? If the Sun were a hollow ball, 1 million Earths would fit inside it.

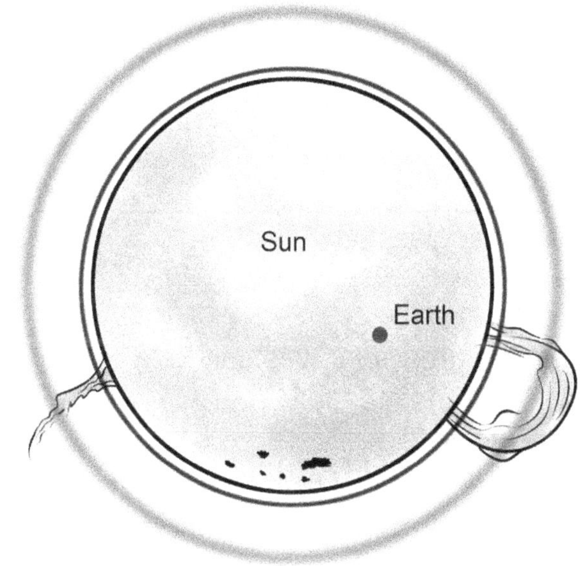

One million Earths could fit inside the Sun. The Sun has 333,000 times the mass of Earth.

Other Stars

Like the Sun, all stars are balls of burning gas. But stars are not all the same size and color. Stars can be 40 times as large as our Sun, or almost as small as Earth. Blue stars are very hot, while red stars are much cooler. In between are white and yellow stars. Our Sun is known as a yellow dwarf star.

The Sun seems larger than other stars in the sky because it is closer to us than any other star. Some stars are so far away that their light takes more than 1,000 years to reach Earth.

Think About It!

1. In what ways does the Sun affect Earth? Use the information from the article and your own ideas to write your answer.

____

____

SAFETY ALERT

Never look at the Sun! Even when you wear sunglasses, sunlight can damage your eyes.

Brain Stretch

All stars have a life cycle. Do some research to find out about the stages in the life cycle of a star. Create an information poster that includes diagrams and labels.

Experiment: Create a Sunset

The Sun looks yellow. Why are sunsets red? Do this activity to find out.

What You Need

- Clear glass bowl
- Water
- Spoon
- Few drops of low-fat milk
- White note paper
- Flashlight

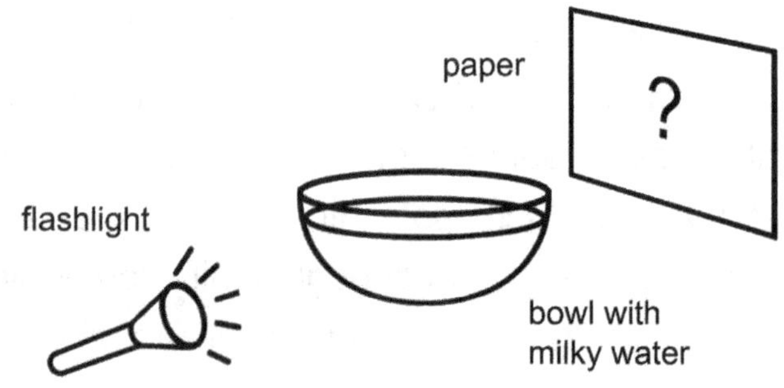

What You Do

1. Fill the bowl with water.
2. Hold up the piece of paper on one side of the bowl. Hold the flashlight on the other side of the bowl.
3. Shine the light through the water so that the light hits the paper. Record what you see.
4. Use the spoon to add a few drops of milk until the water looks cloudy.
5. Repeat steps 2 and 3. Record what you see.

Think About It!

1. What did you see when you shone the light through clear water? (Step 3)

____

____

2. What did you see when you shone the light through milky water? (Step 5)

____

____

3. How is the milky water similar to Earth's atmosphere?

____

____

____

Planets in Our Solar System

There are eight planets orbiting our Sun. Each planet orbits the Sun on its own path. The planets' paths are hundreds of millions of miles (kilometers) apart. At any point in time, the planets are usually all at very different places along their paths. So, the distance between planets is even greater. Earth is so far from the Sun that the Sun's light takes eight minutes to reach our planet.

Each planet spins around as it orbits the Sun. On Earth, this creates night and day as different sides of the planet get sunlight. The time it takes for a planet to orbit the Sun is one year. Earth's year is 365 days long. Other planets have shorter years than Earth and some have much longer years.

Some planets have moons and some have rings. Some have atmosphere, winds, and storms. Huge craters, mountains, and canyons can be seen on some planets. Match each planet to a description below.

Mercury

Mercury is the closest planet to the Sun and is the smallest planet in our solar system. The surface is gray and rocky and has a lot of craters. With almost no atmosphere, it does not have storms, clouds, winds, or rain. With no atmosphere to trap the daytime heat, the temperature can drop 1,112 °F (600 °C) from day to night. No other planet has such an extreme temperature range.

Venus

Venus is about the size of Earth. The temperature on the surface is hot enough to melt lead. In fact, no planet is hotter than Venus. Not even Mercury, which is the planet closest to the Sun. Mercury and Venus are the only two planets that do not have moons orbiting them. Venus is easy to see. It reflects the Sun's light so brightly that some people mistake it for a star.

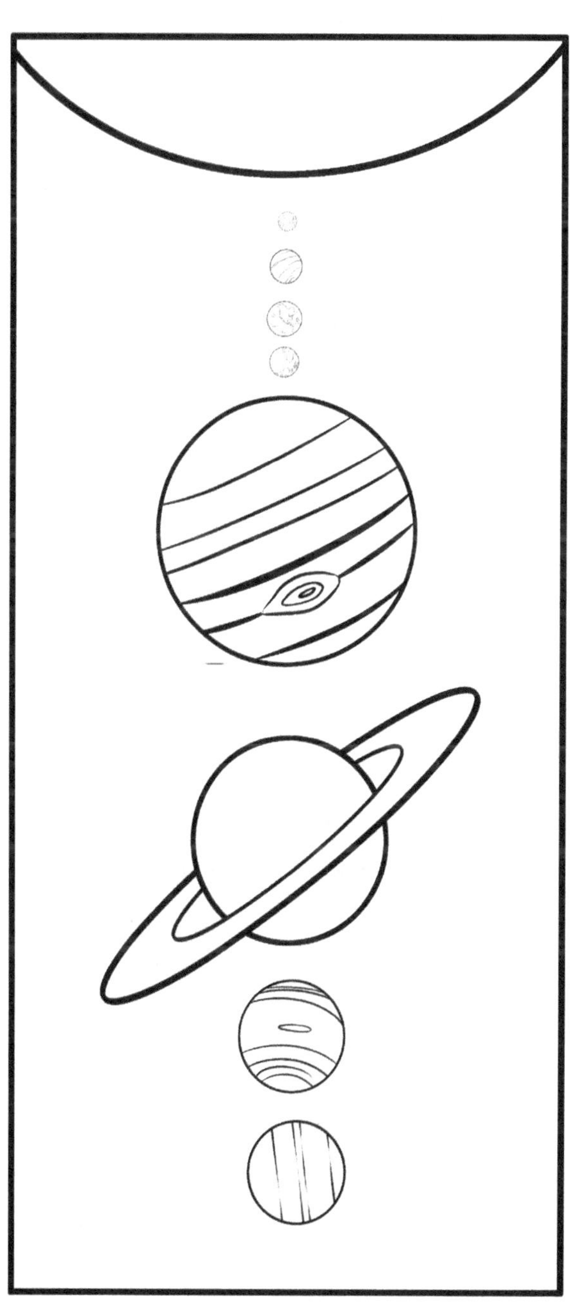

continued next page

Earth

From space, Earth looks blue. That is because oceans cover 70 percent of Earth's surface. Earth is the third planet from the Sun and the largest of the four rocky planets. It is the densest planet. Earth spins on a tilt as it orbits the Sun. This tilt means that half the planet gets more solar energy than the other half. This tilt is the reason Earth has changing seasons.

Mars

Iron in the soil gives the planet a reddish color. Huge dust storms can almost cover the planet. Mars is about half the size of Earth, but has the highest mountain and the largest canyon of any planet. Space probes have looked for life on Mars, but found none. But scientists think the planet may once have been covered in rivers and oceans.

Jupiter

Jupiter is called a gas giant. This planet is so big that all other planets could fit inside it. Jupiter has at least 64 moons—more than any other planet. One moon is larger than Mercury. Jupiter is the fifth planet from the Sun, but can be seen easily from Earth. A space probe showed that Jupiter is circled by faint dark rings made of dust and bits of rock.

Saturn

No other planet has rings so bright. These rings are made of pieces of dust, rock, and ice. Some are as small as a fingernail, others are as big as a house. Some experts think the rings contains materials left over from when Saturn formed. Others think the rings contain pieces of nearby moons, chipped off by meteorites.

Uranus

Uranus is the only planet tilted on its side. Some experts think it may once have been hit by something huge that knocked it on its side. The planet is the third-largest in our solar system and is surrounded by faint rings. Unlike other planets, it has no cloud bands or storms. Uranus is so far from the Sun, that sunlight on Earth is 400 times brighter than the sunlight on Uranus.

Neptune

Neptune is a giant blue ball with wisps of white clouds. The winds blow up to 1,243 mph (2,000 kph) on Neptune. No other planet has faster winds. Neptune is about the same size as Uranus. There are four seasons on Neptune, but each season lasts more than 40 Earth years.

1. Mars has two moons: Phobos and Deimos. How many moons do the four planets closest to the Sun have altogether? _______________________

2. Which planet has the highest-known mountain? _______________________________________

3. Which planet is the hottest? ____

4. Which planet is the smallest? ____

5. Which planet is the largest? ____

6. Which planet is the densest?____

7. Which planet has the greatest daily temperature change? ______________________________

8. Which planet spins on its side? ____

9. Imagine the Sun is the size of a basketball. Now match each planet with an item about its size. (Hint: three pairs of planets are about the same size as each other. For instance, Venus is almost the same size as Earth.)

a) Mercury i) small number cube

b) Venus   ii) gum ball

c) Earth   iii) peppercorn

d) Mars   iv) large marble

e) Jupiter   v) black bean

f) Saturn   vi) kernel of corn

g) Uranus   vii) pea

h) Neptune viii) small marble

Brain Stretch

Here is the order of the planets, starting with the planet closest to the Sun: Mercury, Venus, Earth, Mars, Jupiter, Saturn, Uranus, Neptune. The sentence below can help you remember the order of the planets. The first letter of each word is the first letter of a planet.

My Very Efficient Mother Just Served Us Noodles.

Moons

Did you know there are likely about 140 moons in our solar system? Jupiter has more than 64 moons. Mercury and Venus are the only planets that do not have a moon.

A moon can be any size. Two moons in our solar system are even bigger than Mercury. The second-largest moon is Titan, which orbits Saturn. Scientists are very interested in Titan because its atmosphere seems similar to Earth's long ago. Could there be life there now or sometime in the future?

Our Moon is about one quarter the size of Earth. The surface is covered with boulders and a thick layer of gray dust. There are many large craters and mountain ranges, but no atmosphere. Millions of asteroids, comets, and meteorites have scarred the Moon's surface. There is no wind or rain to wash away these marks, so they remain unchanged for years.

The Moon Affects Life on Earth

The Moon circles Earth, reflecting light from the Sun and pulling on Earth's oceans. Ocean tides are caused by the Moon's gravity pulling the water toward the Moon. Since Earth rotates as this happens, two tides happen every day.

A lunar eclipse occurs when Earth comes between the Sun and the Moon. Earth's shadow makes the whole Moon look red and mysterious.

The Sun and Moon must be exactly opposite each other for a total eclipse. Partial eclipses happen much more often. A few lunar eclipses happen each year. Most can only be seen from certain places on Earth, depending on where the darkest shadow passes.

Phases of the Moon

Do you ever wonder why the Moon looks so bright in the night sky? This is because the surface of the Moon reflects the light from the Sun. The part of the Moon facing the Sun is lit up. The part of the Moon facing away from the Sun is dark. The sunlit part of the moon that we see is what is responsible for the Moon's phases. The phases of the Moon depend on its position in relation to the Sun and Earth. As the Moon makes its way around the Earth, the phases of the Moon change.

"Moons"—Think About It!

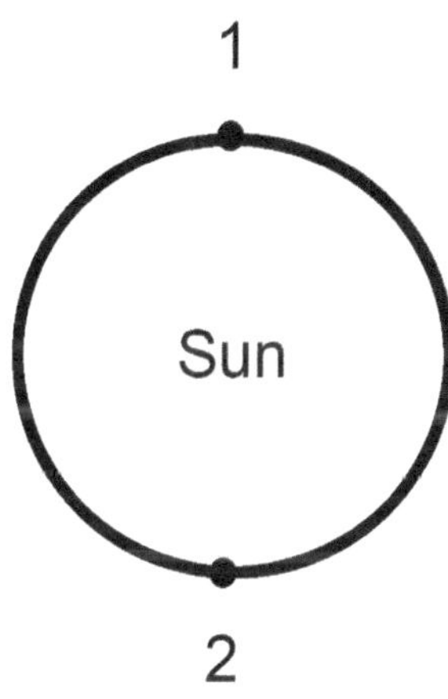

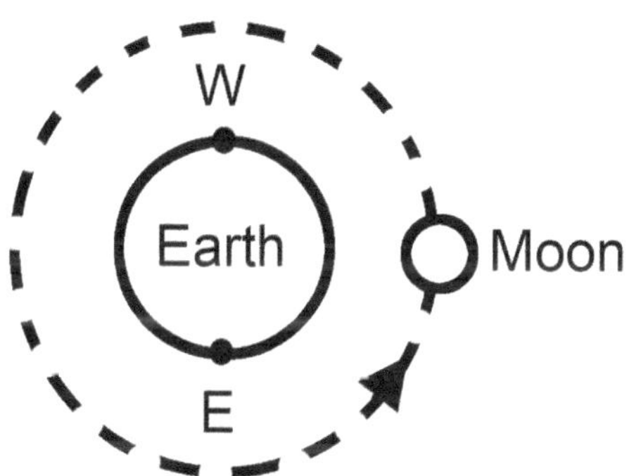

1. On the diagram above, use one color to join point 1 to points E and W. Extend the lines to the Moon. Color between the lines. Use another color to join point 2 to points E and W. Extend the lines to the Moon and color in the shape. Look at the shadow you colored between Earth and the Moon. The area of mixed color is the location of the darkest shadow, and represents a lunar eclipse.

2. Look at the Moon every few nights for about a month. Look in the newspaper to find out what time the Moon should be visible each night. Note what you see.

a) The Moon does not actually change shape. Why does what you see change?

____

____

b) Number the moon pictures below in the order that you saw them.

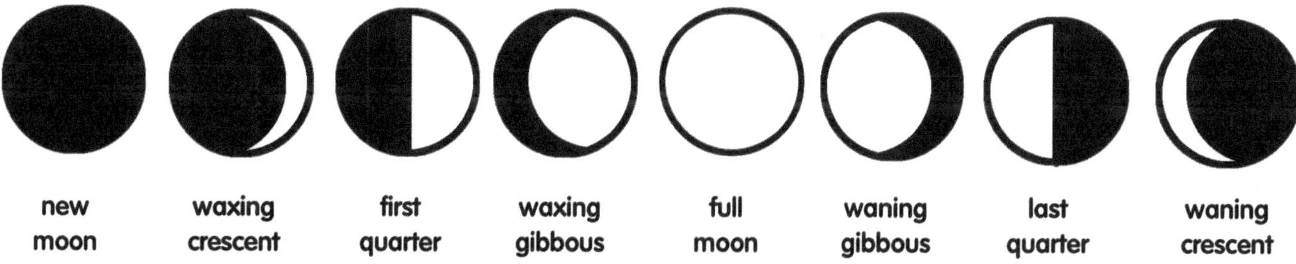

They Came from Outer Space

Comets

You might say a comet is a dirty snowball that orbits the Sun. This snowball is about the size of a small city! As this snowball zooms closer to the Sun, its surface begins to turn into gas. Gas and dust stream out into a tail that can spread out as far as 49,710 mi (80,000 km).

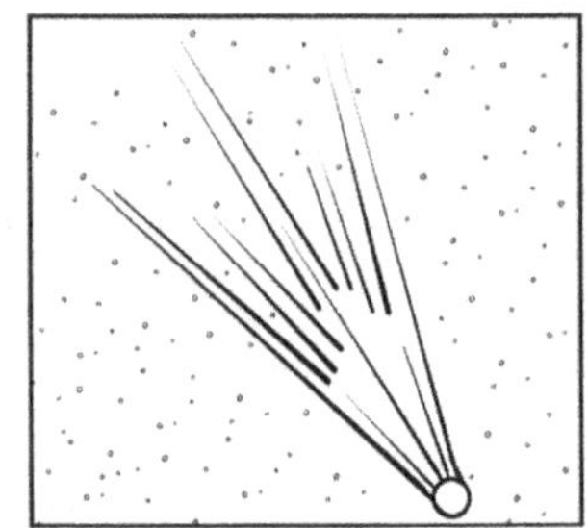

Comets mostly stay farther away from the Sun than our planets are. You will rarely see a comet unless you use a telescope or binoculars. Halley's Comet is the most famous comet. It swings by Earth about every 75 years. You will have to wait until 2062 to see it again.

Asteroids

These space rocks may be shaped like balls, lumpy slabs, or bricks. You find asteroids circling the Sun in the Asteroid Belt, a band that lies between the planets Mars and Jupiter.

The biggest asteroid is bigger than many American states. One asteroid even has its own moon. Most asteroids are only about the size of a house. You need binoculars to seem them.

Meteoroids

Small chunks of asteroids or old comets may become meteoroids. When these rocky bits enter Earth's atmosphere, they become meteors. Ever seen shooting stars? Then you have seen meteors. They burn up and shoot out fiery trails as they fall. If a meteor hits our planet, it gets a new name: meteorite.

Meteors are tiny. Most are as small as grains of sand and few get as big as baseballs. At certain times of year, many meteors streak through the night sky in a meteor shower. You can see them just by gazing up on a clear, dark night.

Think About It!

1. Arrange these in order from largest to smallest: asteroid, meteoroid, comet.

____

2. Research one meteor shower using other resources and explain its name.

____

____

"

Experiment: Mass of Meteorites

Find out whether metal meteorites are heavier than stone meteorites of the same size.

What You Need

- A stone a little smaller than a golf ball
- 200 nickels
- 2 c (250 ml) measuring cup
- Warm water
- 2 small yogurt containers

What You Do

1. Put the stone in the measuring cup and pour in water up to the 1 c (250 ml) mark.

2. Remove the stone without spilling any water. Place the stone in one of the yogurt containers.

3. Record the level of the water in the measuring cup.

4. Add nickels to the water until the level is back up to the 1 c (250 ml) mark. Now you have measured a volume of nickels equal to the stone.

5. Carefully pour out the water and place the nickels in the other yogurt container. Now the two yogurt containers hold stone and metal with the same volumes.

6. Hold a container in each hand. Which container feels heavier? Use a scale to weigh each container to find out. Record which container is heavier.

Think About It!

1. Calculate the volume of the stone: 1 c – new level of water = volume of the stone.

____

2. Which felt heavier: the stone or the metal? _______________________________________

3. Which weighed more: the stone or the metal? _______________________________________

4. What does this tell you about stone and metal asteroids?

____

____

5. How do you think the mass of a similarly sized comet compares? Explain your thinking.

____

____

Explore the Night Sky

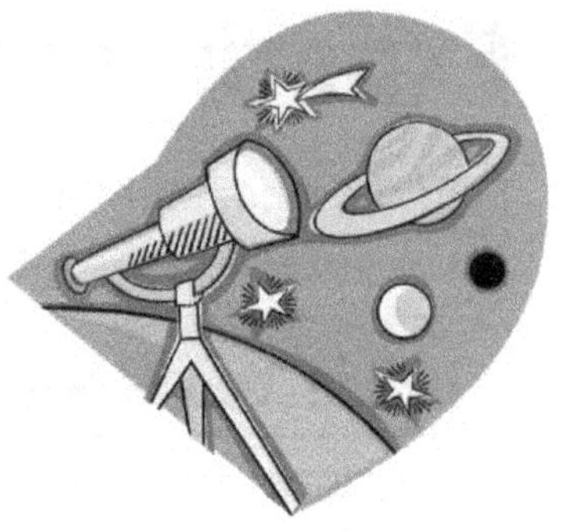

On the clearest and darkest night, you might be able to see 2,500 stars in the sky. You might also see a cloudy path across the sky. That is the faint glow from the other 300 billion stars in our Milky Way galaxy. You can also see some of the planets in our solar system. With binoculars or a telescope, you may even catch a glimpse of the Andromeda galaxy.

Venus is easy to see in our sky. It reflects the Sun's light so brightly that people can mistake it for a star. Mars and Jupiter can be easy to spot—sometimes only the Moon and Venus are brighter in the night sky. Look for Mercury early in the evening or in the early morning, when the Sun is below the horizon.

Have you ever imagined that the clouds look like animals? Sometimes people connect the dots and imagine that the stars make shapes, too. Many cultures have traditional stories about the shapes they imagine in the starry sky. Some stories are about magical animals. Others are about ancient battles, or gods.

Think About It!

1. a) Go outside on a starry night and draw what you see.

Date:_____________________ Time:______________ Direction:_______________________

b) Use a star chart to identify what you saw. Add labels to your drawing. What planets did you see? Did you see any satellites, such as the International Space Station?

c) Compare drawings with a classmate. Did you both see the same stars and shapes? Explain any differences.

2. a) Find someone to tell you a story about the stars. Or, ask a librarian to help you find stories from around the world. Record the story. You might write it down or use a camera or voice recorder.

b) How many different stories about the stars did your class collect? Create a podcast or puppet show to share your favorite stories.

Eye in the Sky

There are quite a few telescopes in space, but none is more famous than the Hubble Space Telescope. It has beamed back to Earth an incredible amount of information about the other planets in our solar system, as well as data about stars and galaxies.

Edwin P. Hubble was an astronomer—a scientist who studies stars, planets, and galaxies. He made important discoveries about the universe in the early 1900s. The telescope named after him was launched by the Space Shuttle *Discovery* on April 24, 1990. The Hubble Space Telescope is about the size of a large school bus, and it weighs approximately 12 tons (11 metric tons), or as much as two elephants.

Beyond Earth's Atmosphere

Space telescopes like Hubble are very important because they provide scientists with high-quality images that cannot be taken from Earth. Our planet's atmosphere prevents telescopes on Earth from taking clear and detailed photos of distant objects in space. Space telescopes are outside Earth's atmosphere, so they can capture images that are much clearer. Astronomers can learn much more from photos taken in space.

Hubble's First Photos

Hubble runs on power provided by two large solar panels. To create images, Hubble uses a digital camera, which takes photos the same way a cell phone does. Using radio waves, the telescope sends images back to Earth.

If a camera is not held very still when taking a picture, the photo comes out blurry. Hubble has technology that helps it "lock on" to a star, keeping the telescope steady while it is creating an image. Scientists waited eagerly for Hubble to send back its first photos. They wondered what they might learn from crisp, clear photos taken in space. When the images finally came, scientists were disappointed. The photos were blurry!

Problem Solved

Since Hubble was taking photos outside Earth's atmosphere, and it had technology to keep the telescope steady while it created images, why were the images blurry?

continued next page 

Hubble has two mirrors that it uses to capture images. Scientists figured out that the photos were blurry because of a problem with one of the mirrors. But how could they fix the problem when Hubble was orbiting Earth?

Luckily, Hubble was designed to be serviced by astronauts. In 1993, astronauts were sent on a mission to correct the problem with the mirror. The mission was a success. Since then, four more space shuttle missions have repaired, replaced, and upgraded Hubble's systems.

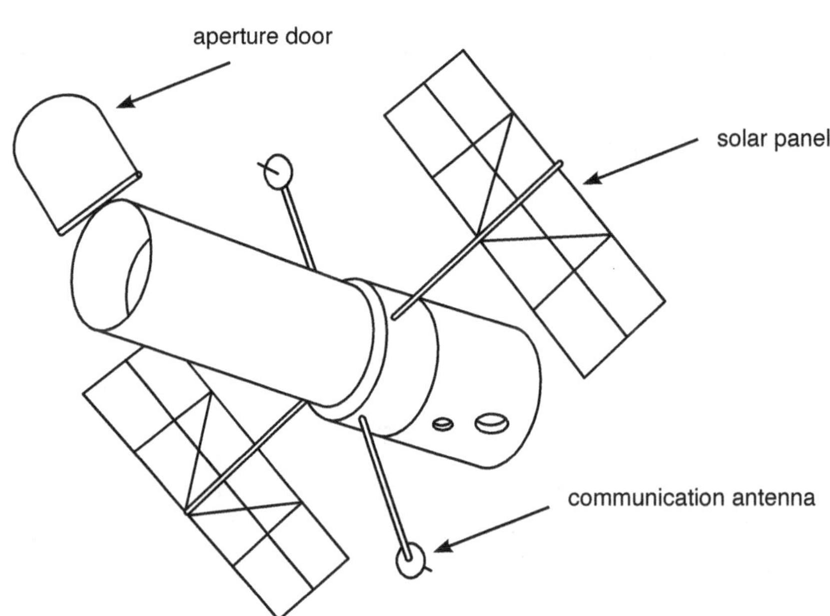

The aperture door can close to prevent light from the Sun from damaging the telescope. Hubble's mirrors are located inside the telescope.

Scientific Breakthroughs

The information that Hubble has beamed back to Earth over the years has led to many scientific breakthroughs. Scientists know that the universe is constantly expanding, but data from Hubble has allowed them to calculate how fast it is expanding. Hubble has also helped astronomers estimate that the universe is 13 to 14 billion years old.

From Hubble, we have learned that there are moons circling Pluto. Astronomers had never seen them before. Images Hubble sent back also helped scientists understand how galaxies and planets form. However, there are some things Hubble cannot do. For example, it does not observe the Sun because the extremely bright light from this star might damage the telescope's sensitive equipment.

Hubble was originally planned to continue operating only until 2014. Now scientists say it may last until 2030 or 2040. What new discoveries will scientists make, thanks to the Hubble Space Telescope?

continued next page

Look Up

You may be able to see Hubble as it orbits Earth. Check online to discover when it will next be passing over where you live. Look up into the sky on a clear night. Hubble circles Earth every 96 minutes, so if you can see it, it will look like a fast-moving star.

"Eye in the Sky"—Think About It!

1. Why are space telescopes an important tool for astronomers?

____

____

____

2. The article says that the Hubble Space Telescope was designed to be "serviced" by astronauts. What exactly does the author mean by "serviced"? Use details from the text to support your response.

____

____

____

3. Hubble has taken photos of Pluto, which is very far away, but it has not taken photos of Mercury (the planet closest to the Sun), which is much closer than Pluto. Use information from the article to explain why Hubble has not taken photos of Mercury.

____

____

____

Astronauts and Space Travel

In space you do not feel gravity. It is extremely cold, and there is no atmosphere to breathe or to protect you from the Sun's radiation. It takes enormous energy to get there, and you have to take everything you need with you—even the air. Outer space is an extreme environment.

The first person in space orbited Earth for less than two hours in 1957. Less than 40 years later, another astronaut spent a record-setting 438 days in space. Space travel has changed a lot since then. Between 1969 and 1972, 12 astronauts set foot on the Moon. These are the only times a human has landed anywhere other than Earth.

After leaving Earth, life support is the most important function of a space craft. It must clean the air for astronauts to breathe and provide heat. It must also protect the contents from the Xrays and other radiation coming from the Sun. All things used in space are designed for the low gravity. Tools are attached to surfaces so they do not float away. Even drinking becomes difficult. You do not think about it, but gravity keeps the drink in your glass. Without gravity, the drink floats in a ball. Meals must be eaten from containers that keep the food from floating away. Equipment must be protected from floating crumbs, too.

Gravity on Earth also makes your muscles work hard. This exercise helps the blood spread throughout your body. In space, blood does not circulate as well. Lack of exercise makes the body lose muscle and bone mass. Astronauts have to strap themselves into exercise equipment to keep fit without floating away!

Brain Stretch

What do you think are four character traits someone needs to have to become an astronaut? Justify your thinking for each character trait.

"Astronauts and Space Travel"—Think About It!

1. List 10 items you would need in space. Give a reason why you want to take each item.

\
\
\
\
\
\
\
\
\
\

2. What are the most important features to have on a spacecraft? Remember, the spacecraft has to provide everything an astronaut will need while in space.

\
\
\
\
\
\

Brain Stretch

Some of the things we use on Earth were invented for space travel. Heat cameras, insulation, multivitamins, and cordless tools are just a few examples. Use books or Internet resources to learn about one such invention. Create a demonstration to show people how to use it on Earth.

Other Spacecraft

Satellites

Space travel began with a satellite called Sputnik (Russian for "traveling companion"). This satellite was launched in 1957. It provided information about Earth's atmosphere. Today there are about 3,000 satellites orbiting Earth. They carry equipment that connects phones, television, and the Internet. Some satellites watch the weather, some send data to GPS units, others take pictures of Earth and the stars. One big satellite is a telescope.

Probes

The space probe Pioneer 10 was launched in 1972. It was the first spacecraft to fly close to Jupiter. The probe sent back the first close-up images of Jupiter, then continued out of our solar system. Pioneer 10's last signal was received in 2003. The probe is on a 2-million-year journey to a star.

Some probes land on planets. Probes such as rovers move, but stationary landers do not move. In 1997, the rover Sojourner landed on Mars and became the first rover to land on another planet. For more than two months, it sent back images of Mars. It also sent information about chemicals in the rocks and soil, and about the weather on the red planet.

Space Telescopes

Space telescopes are another way scientists can learn about the solar system. The Hubble Telescope was launched into orbit around Earth in 1990. The telescope has beamed back information about the universe's past and future. Hubble takes clearer pictures than a telescope on Earth because there is no atmosphere in space to warp the image. This telescope is solar powered and can be repaired in space.

International Space Station (ISS)

This is the largest and most expensive spacecraft ever built. The space station is one of Earth's artificial satellites, but it is also home to crews of astronauts. It is so big that you can see its glow as it crosses the night sky. The first part of the ISS was launched in 1998. Now it has solar panels for power, living quarters, and science labs.

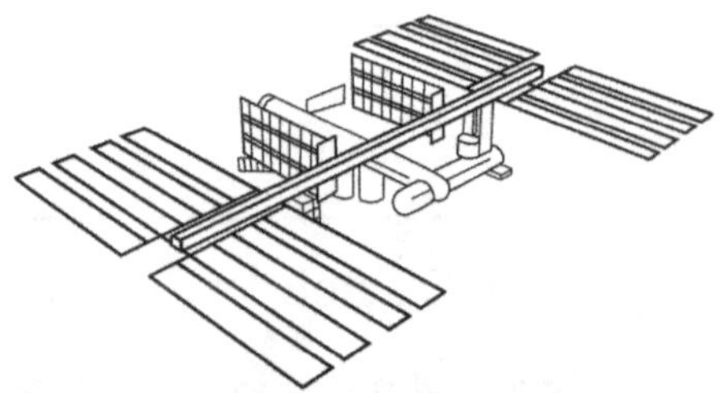

International Space Station (ISS)

Space shuttles carry food, water, equipment, and crew members back and forth between Earth and the ISS. The United States, Russia, Canada, Japan, and some European countries have all contributed to the station. The space station may one day be a launching base for a mission to the Moon, Mars, and beyond.

"Other Spacecraft"—Think About It!

1. What are the pros and cons of orbiting spacecraft and spacecraft that land on a planet?

2. Imagine designing a land rover to explore a new planet. List three things you have to plan for in the design. Describe two things you will need the rover to do.

3. A lander is a spacecraft that lands on another planet. What advantages does a rover have over a stationary lander?

Brain Stretch

What do you think when you see the lights of an airplane in the sky at night? It may be the International Space Station (ISS). You can often see satellites in the night sky. They reflect sunlight just like the planets do.

Go outside just after sunset or right before sunrise. Those two times are when the ISS is lit by the Sun but you are in darkness. You cannot see the ISS at other times. Look online to get more information about the best place to look for the ISS.

Astronaut Research Report

Research one of these famous astronauts. Write a report about their early life and achievements. Include some interesting facts.

- Buzz Aldrin
- Kathryn Sullivan
- Ellen Ochoa
- Yuri Gagarin
- Neil Armstrong
- Guion Bluford, Jr.
- Mae Jemison
- Alan Shepard
- Edward H. White
- Eileen Collins
- John Glenn, Jr.
- James Lovell
- Sally Ride
- Franklin Chang-Díaz
- Ellison Shoji Onizuka

Neil Armstrong

Name ____

Date of Birth: ____

____

____

____

____

____

____

____

____

____

____

____

____

Space Technology

Space travel has changed your life in ways you probably never imagined. From your sunglasses to the shoes you wear hiking, space technology touches your life.

How were these devices first used in space?

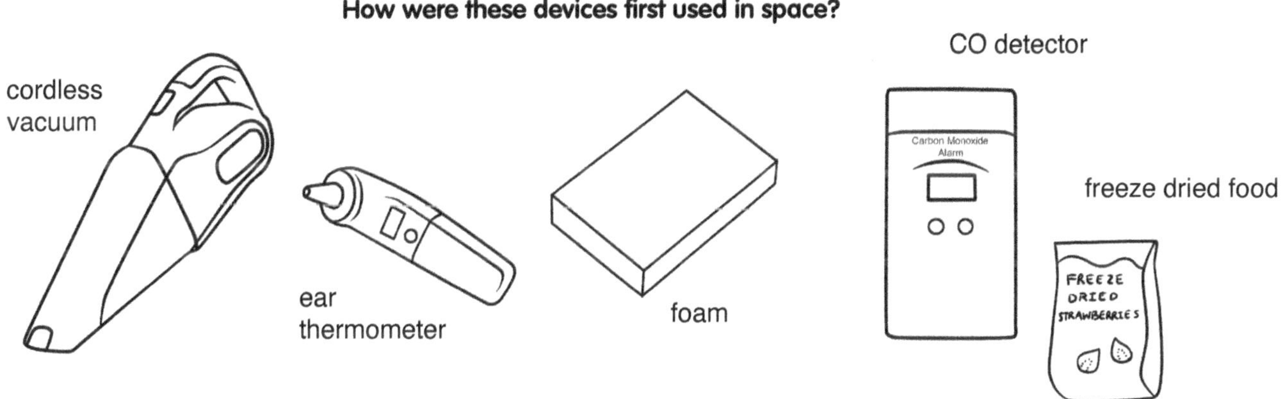

You likely already know that radio and television signals are transmitted around our planet by satellite. Other satellites help with navigation. Many cars now have global positioning systems (GPS), which are navigation systems that use satellites. Other products include the scratchproof coating on sunglasses, and medical technology. Insulin crystals (to fight diabetes) were grown in space. The technology used for space shuttle fuel pumps is now used in artificial hearts.

Space technology is great but it costs a lot. It takes an incredible amount of money to put an astronaut into space. Just a toilet on the ISS costs $19 million. Also, astronauts' dirty clothes cannot be cleaned, so these expensive garments are just thrown away. Is this the best way for a government to spend its money?

Here on Earth, money is desperately needed to improve medical care and other services. We also need more money to help the environment. Is it right to spend money on space research when the money is needed elsewhere? Are space programs just a way for one country to pretend it is better than another because it has more advanced space technology?

Space travel also creates a lot of pollution. Launching a spacecraft uses a lot of fuel. On Earth, people are trying to save fuel. Space research also adds to the garbage orbiting Earth or eventually landing on our planet. Some pieces are as large as a car. Even bits as small as flecks of paint can damage other spacecraft because of the speeds at which they travel.

The worst outcome of space research can be disastrous. Although every aspect is carefully planned, sometimes tragedies happen. In 1986, the Space Shuttle *Challenger* blew up shortly after takeoff. Then in 2003, the shuttle *Columbia* broke apart as it reentered Earth's atmosphere. In both cases, all seven crew members were killed.

"Space Technology"—Think About It!

1. a) How do you feel about space technology and exploration?

____

____

____

____

____

b) What are the benefits? Do the benefits outweigh the costs? Explain your thinking.

____

____

____

____

____

2. Do you think life on Earth would be better or worse without space travel? Explain your thinking.

____

____

____

____

____

3. Imagine exploring the ocean in a submarine. How is this similar to life in space?

____

____

____

____

continued next page

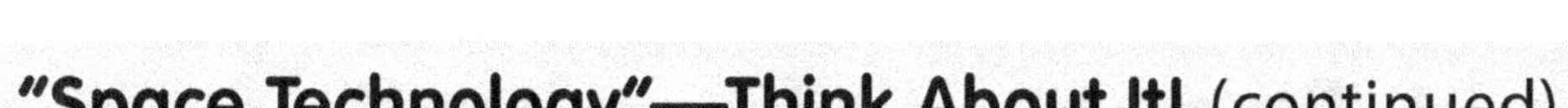

4. Space technology has changed the foods we eat. There are six main ways food is stored for astronauts to eat onboard the space shuttle. Match each method with its description.

a) Fresh

i) Food is freeze-dried to remove water. Water is replaced before eating.

b) Intermediate Moisture

ii) Food with some water removed; water is not replaced before eating.

c) Irradiated

iii) Food is cooked and packed in foil pouches. The food is sterilized by radiation so it can be kept at room temperature.

d) Natural

iv) Food is heated to kill bacteria so it can be stored at room temperature.

e) Rehydratable

v) Food is ready to eat and stored in flexible pouches.

f) Thermostabilized

vi) Food is not preserved so it must be eaten quickly.

5. Tell how you use space technology in your daily life.

____

____

____

____

Did You Know?

The robotic Canadarm was a remote-controlled manipulator that was attached to a space shuttle. There, it could capture, repair, and launch satellites, position astronauts, help hold equipment, and move cargo. The jointed Canadarm was launched in 1981. It could move objects weighing as much as 66,139 lb (30,000 kg). In 2001, Canadarm2 was launched. The new device played an important role in the building of the International Space Station (ISS).

Animals in Space—Fair or Not?

Cats, dogs, frogs, guinea pigs, and monkeys. Did you know all of these animals have been launched into space?

Before sending anyone into space, no one knew how traveling so far from Earth's surface would affect humans. Could astronauts survive the launch and re-entry? What about surviving space radiation? What effect would microgravity have on them?

Scientists knew that there were no machines they could launch that would give them all the answers they needed. They decided to send other animals to test the trip.

In 1957, Russian scientists launched the dog Laika (the name means "Barker" in Russian), who became the first animal to orbit Earth. A dog was chosen because scientists felt it could endure the long stretches of inactivity involved in space travel. Sadly, Laika died when her spacecraft overheated.

Today, animals are still sent into space to take part in experiments. For instance, does floating confuse animals? Laura Lewis, from NASA Ames Institutional Animal Care and Use Committee tested that question. She found that mice adapted very quickly to floating. Within minutes, the mice were grooming themselves and eating.

Think About It!

1. Do you think it is acceptable to send animals into space? Why? If not, are there any times when you think it might be alright? If so, explain them.

____

____

____

____

____

____

____

____

Those Puzzling Planets

Solve the clues to complete the crossword on the next page.

Across

2. A natural satellite
4. Path made by something in space as it circles another object
5. The red planet
7. Planet known for its huge rings
10. Planet mostly covered in water
11. Seasons on this planet last 40 Earth years
13. Planet that spins on its side
14. Lack of atmosphere gives this planet extreme daily temperatures
17. Biggest object in our solar system
18. Objects orbiting the Sun that can be as large as a state

Down

1. Made up of the Sun and planets
3. Made by connecting the dots of stars in the sky
6. Its ice melts into a huge tail that streaks across the night sky
8. These showers are named for the constellation you see them near
9. Planet with strong acid rain
12. An enormous gas planet
15. Famous Canadian part of the space shuttle
16. The Milky Way is one

Brain Stretch

The order of the planets outward from the Sun is Mercury, Venus, Earth, Mars, Jupiter, Saturn, Uranus, Neptune. To remember this, make up a sentence in which each word starts with the first letter of each planet, in order.

continued next page ☞

Use the clues on page 89 to complete this crossword.

STEM-Related Occupations

To learn more about some of these occupations visit the following websites:

www.sciencebuddies.org/science-engineering-careers

https://kids.usa.gov/watch-videos/index.shtml

Accountant
Aerospace Engineer
Agricultural Engineer
Agricultural Technician
Aircraft Mechanic and
    Service Technician
Animal Breeder
Animal Trainer
Animator
Anthropologist
Architect
Astronaut
Astronomer
Athletic Trainer
Audio Engineer
Audiologist
Automotive Mechanic
Biochemical Engineer
Biochemist/Biophysicist
Biologist
Biology Teacher
Biomedical Engineer
Business Owner
Cardiovascular Technician
Carpenter
Chef
Chemical Engineer
Chemical Technician
Chemistry Teacher
Chiropractor
Civil Engineer
Civil Engineering Technician
Climate Change Analyst
Clinical Psychologist
Computer Engineer
Computer Programmer
Computer Systems Analyst
Construction Manager
Counselling Psychologist
Dietetic Technician

Dietitian and Nutritionist
Doctor
Electrical Engineering Technician
Electrician
Electronics Engineer
Emergency Medical Technician
Environmental Engineer
Environmental Engineering Technician
Environmental Restoration Planner
Environmental Scientist
Epidemiologist
Fire-Prevention Engineer
Fish and Game Worker
Food Science Technician
Food Scientist and Technologist
Forest and Conservation Technician
Forest and Conservation Worker
Geoscientist
Graphic Designer
Hydrologist
Industrial Engineer
Interior Designer
Landscape Architect
Manufacturing Engineer
Marine Architect
Marine Biologist
Math Teacher
Mechanical Engineer
Mechanical Engineering Technician
Medical Lab Technician
Medical Scientist
Meteorologist
Microbiologist
Microsystems Engineer
Mining and Geological Engineer
Molecular and Cellular Biologist
Neurologist
Nuclear Engineer
Nursery and Greenhouse Manager
Nutritionist

Occupational Health and Safety Specialist
Optical Engineer
Optometrist
Paleontologist
Patent Lawyer
Pathologist
Park Ranger
Petroleum Engineer
Pharmacist
Physical Therapist
Physician
Physician Assistant
Physicist
Pilot
Psychologist
Registered Nurse
Respiratory Therapist
Robotics Engineer
Robotics Technician
School Psychologist
Seismologist
Software Developer (Applications)
Software Developer (Systems Software)
Soil and Plant Scientist
Soil and Water Conservationist
Space Scientist
Speech-Language Pathologist
Statistician
Transportation Engineer
Transportation Planner
Urban Planner
Veterinarian
Video Game Designer
Volcanologist
Water/Wastewater Engineer
Wind Energy Engineer
X-ray Technician
Zookeeper
Zoologist
Wildlife Biologist

Science, Technology, Engineering, and Mathematics (STEM) Occupation Brochure

Create a brochure about a STEM-related occupation.

STEP 1: Plan Your Brochure

❑ Fold a piece of paper the same way your brochure will be folded. Before writing the brochure, plan the layout in pencil. Sections of the brochure should include
- Job description
- Training or degree needed
- Work environment
- How the occupation relates to STEM
- Interesting facts

❑ Write the heading for each section where you would like it to be in the brochure.

❑ Plan where graphics or pictures will be placed in the brochure.

STEP 2: Complete a Draft

❑ Research information for each section of your brochure. Check your facts.

❑ Read your draft for meaning, then add, delete, or change words to make your writing better.

❑ Plan what illustrations or graphics you will put into your brochure.

STEP 3: Checklist

❑ My brochure is neat and well organized.

❑ My brochure has accurate information.

❑ My brochure has pictures or graphics that go well with the information.

❑ I checked the spelling.

❑ I checked the punctuation.

❑ My brochure is attractive.

What Does an Engineer Do?

Engineers are people who build all types of things that make our world work better. Many of the things you see and use every day were created by engineers. Some engineers work with chemicals to create new textiles, more flexible plastics, and stronger building materials. Others work in cities to build roads, bridges, and skyscrapers. Some engineers make medical supplies for hospitals, technology for space travel, and find new and safer ways to clean up the environment. Engineers can build or create just about anything!

There are many different types of engineers.

Civil engineers make structures and systems that help cities and industries work and grow. They build bridges, highways, railways, skyscrapers, engines and machines, airplanes and rocket ships.

Chemical engineers work with chemicals to find new ways of producing and improving the goods we use. They make such things as safer foods, softer and warmer clothing, new types of plastics, and textiles that do not catch fire.

Environmental engineers work to find ways of solving problems that affect animals, plants, and humans. They find ways to clean up polluted water and air, and to safely dispose of toxic wastes to make Earth cleaner and safer.

Audio engineers work with sound, and the programs and equipment that create, record, and share that sound. They create the music, audio books, and radio programs we listen to. They also create the fun and exciting sound effects and music for movies, television shows, and video games.

Computer engineers create programs to run your computer and to make it more useful and fun. They also help provide hospitals with programs that control X-ray machines and keep track of patient information.

Optical engineers make technologies that use and control light. These engineers create eyeglasses, camera lenses, televisions, telescopes, microscopes, lasers, solar cells, and broadband networks that bring the Internet into homes.

Electrical engineers work with electricity. They help build power stations. They also design the power lines that carry the electricity to where it is needed. Electricity helps your furnace to heat your home, and powers your lights, phone, computer, television, and appliances. Electricity also powers streetlights, traffic lights, and entire cities.

Can you imagine what life would be like without paved roads, radios, computers, phones, television, refrigerators, plastics, apartment buildings, or electric lights? Without the hard work of so many types of engineers, our lives would be very different!

"What Does an Engineer Do?"—Think About It!

1. What type of engineer would you like to be? Explain why.

2. How do engineers help people in their daily lives?

Think Like an Engineer!

An engineer is a person who designs and build things. Engineers want to understand how and why things work. Engineers try different ideas, learn from their mistakes, then try again. Engineers call these steps the design process.

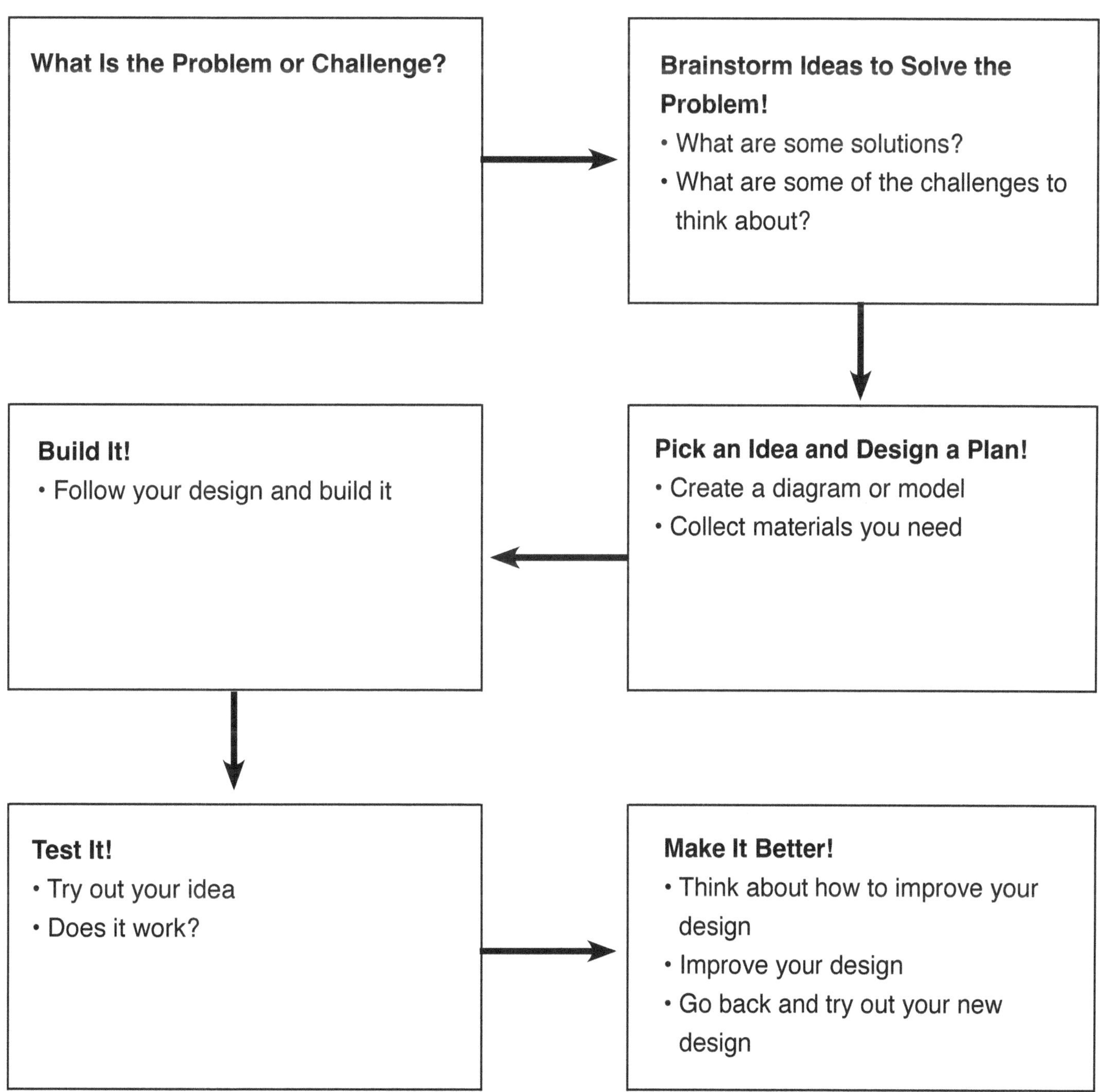

Remember to be patient. Take your time to figure things out.

The Design Process

1. What is the problem or challenge?

____

____

____

2. Brainstorm! What are some solutions? List any possible challenges to think about.

____

____

____

____

____

____

____

continued next page

3. Pick a design idea! Draw and label a diagram of your design. Add notes about your design plan.

____

____

____

continued next page

4. Get ready! What materials do you need? Collect the materials you will need.

____

____

____

____

____

____

Other notes:

____

____

____

____

____

____

continued next page

5. Test it! Build your design and try it out.

Did it work?   Yes ☐   A little ☐   No ☐

6. Make it better! How can you make your design better?

____

____

____

7. Go back! Try your design out again. What happened?

____

____

____

8. What do you wonder about?

____

____

____

9. What are you proud of?

____

____

Incredible Bionics

Bionics is the science of replacing a body part, or improving the function of a body part, with a device created by humans. Scientists have successfully used bionic devices to help many people with certain types of disabilities or diseases.

Creating Artificial Body Parts

The first step in designing a bionic organ or limb (arm or leg) is to understand how the body part works. The next step is to understand how that body part works with other parts of the body. With this information, it is often possible to create a bionic body part that functions like the part that is missing or not working properly.

For instance, scientists have developed an artificial pancreas. The pancreas is an organ that produces insulin, which controls the amount of glucose (a type of sugar) in a person's blood. People get diabetes when their pancreas does not produce enough insulin. Throughout the day, an artificial pancreas measures how much glucose is in a person's blood, and releases insulin when necessary.

Kidneys filter waste out of the blood and help the body get rid of extra fluid. Some people whose kidneys do not work properly must go to a hospital, up to three times a week for four hours each visit. There they are hooked up to a special machine that cleans their blood the same way kidneys do. It is a kind of artificial organ. Scientists have now developed a bionic kidney that is small enough to wear on a belt. People who have this device no longer need to spend hours each week in a hospital.

More Amazing Bionics

A bionic eye is a tiny camera that records visual information, then converts the information into electronic signals. The camera sends these signals wirelessly to tiny devices that a surgeon has placed in someone's eye. Bionic eyes cannot give normal vision to people who are blind, but they can help people who have certain kinds of vision problems.

If you watch closely how people walk, you will notice that everyone walks a bit differently. A bionic knee can sense how a person walks. Then it adjusts itself so the person can walk in a way that appears natural. The bionic knee can also sense what kind of ground a person is walking over and adjust itself to make walking easier.

continued next page

Would you believe that scientists have even created an electronic tongue? It does not replace a person's tongue, but food companies use the device. As they create foods, companies use different ingredients to create a specific flavor. An electronic tongue can test foods to make sure the flavor is exactly the same every time.

Printing Body Parts

Scientists are now using three-dimensional (3-D) printers to create artificial body parts. In 3-D printing, the printer lays down thin layers of rubber and plastic on top of each other to create a 3-D object.

Using 3-D printers, doctors can now make identical copies of the body's organs. These copies do not function like human organs, but doctors use them to plan how to perform surgeries on organs.

People who have lost part of an arm or leg often replace the missing part with an artificial part. It can be a challenge to find an artificial part that fits well. Scientists can use a device called a 3-D scanner to take extremely accurate measurements of the part of the limb that remains. These measurements are sent to a computer that is connected to a 3-D printer. The printer creates an artificial part that fits perfectly.

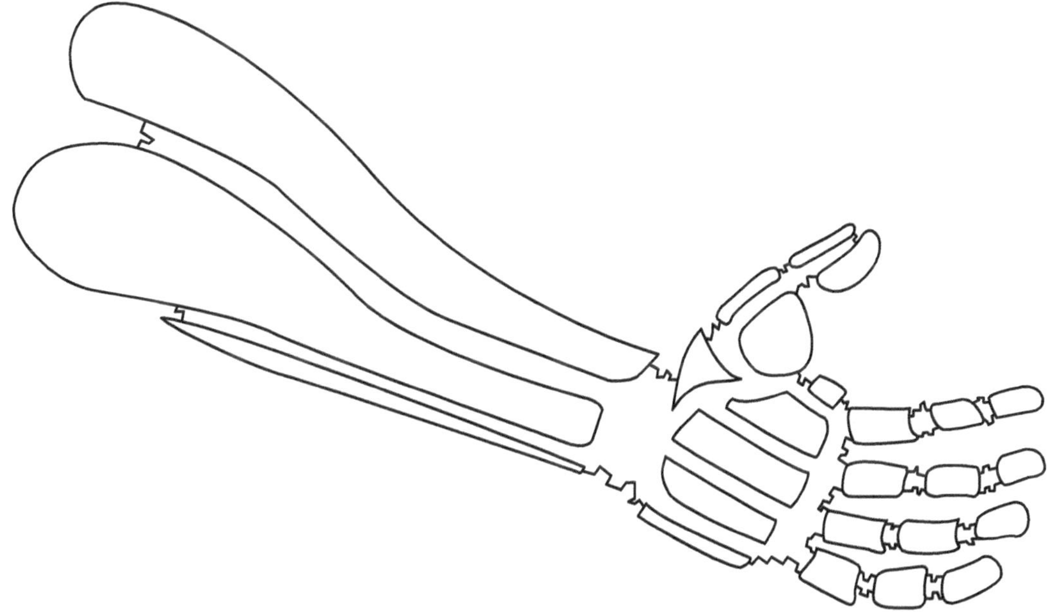

This bionic hand can be created on a 3-D printer, although the electronics that go inside cannot. Using a 3-D printer for the outside of the hand makes it more affordable.

continued next page

Bionics of the Future

Scientists continue to work on new ways to use bionics. For example, if you are having a problem with your heart, a doctor might prescribe a drug. When you take the drug, it circulates through your whole body. The drug might help your heart, but it could have negative effects on other parts of your body. Scientists are developing artificial cells that can deliver drugs directly where they are needed, so they do not affect other parts of the body.

People who need an organ transplant often wait a long time for a suitable organ to become available. Scientists hope that future 3-D printers will be able to create working organs that can be used for transplants. How could this be possible? Instead of using rubber and plastic to create organs, the printers would use human cells.

"Incredible Bionics"—Think About It!

1. Is a hearing aid an example of a bionic device? Why or why not?

____

____

____

____

2. What is the most important difference between a healthy human organ and an organ created with a 3-D printer?

____

____

____

____

"Incredible Bionics"—Think About It! (continued)

3. Do you think it would be useful for scientists who create bionic body parts and scientists who create robots to share their discoveries? Why or why not?

The World Wide Web

The Beginning of the World Wide Web

Tim Berners-Lee is a British computer scientist and physicist (a scientist who studies matter and energy). In 1980, he was working at a physics lab in Geneva, Switzerland. He often needed to access information on the computers of other scientists he was working with. This was not easy to do.

Tim's computer was connected to the other computers in the lab, but he had to log in to each computer he wanted to access. If the computer was using software he was not familiar with, he had to learn how to use the software so he could get the information he needed. Tim became more and more frustrated with this way of sharing information. He knew there had to be a better way.

When Tim thought of a way to solve this problem, he saw that his solution could be useful outside of the lab, too. The Internet had already been invented. It connected millions of computers, and the number was growing quickly. Tim's idea could make it easier for all these computers to share information over the Internet.

Tim's idea became the World Wide Web (often called the "Web"), which was launched on August 6, 1991. Going online would never be the same.

The Web and the Internet

What is the difference between the Web and the Internet? Some people think they are the same thing, but that is not true. First, it is important to understand what a computer network is.

A computer network consists of two or more computers that are connected, or linked. For example, the computers in a school or office building might be connected in a network. A computer in a network can share information with any other computer in the same network.

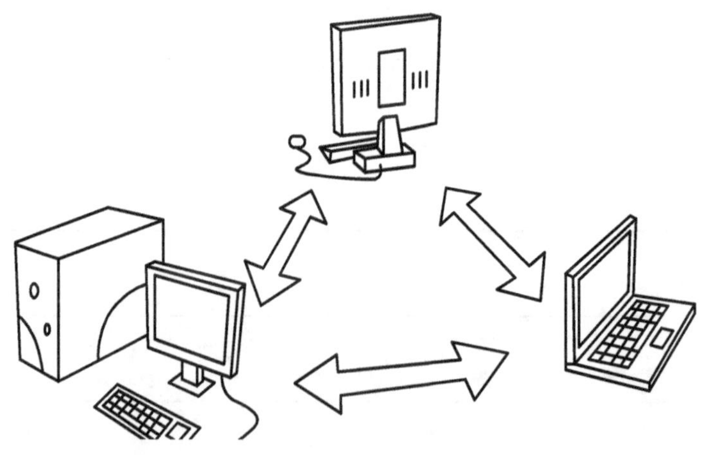

Computers connected in a network can share information with one another.

continued next page 

The Internet is also a network, but instead of connecting individual computers, it connects computer networks all over the world. The Web is a way to access information that is available through the Internet.

Key Technologies in the Web

Tim invented three technologies that make the Web work:

Uniform Resource Locator (URL): A URL is also known as a "Web address." This is what you type into the window of your Web browser (such as Google Chrome, Firefox, or Safari) when you know what Web page you want to go to. Each page of a website has its own URL. Your computer uses the URL to find the Web page you want.

HyperText Markup Language (HTML): HTML consists of short codes (called "tags") that tell a computer how to display text. For example, if you are creating a Web page and you want some parts of the text to appear in italics, you use the HTML tag for italics. There are also HTML tags that let you control the font and color of the text. If you want to create a link people can click on to go to the next page on your website—or even to someone else's website—HTML lets you do this.

HyperText Transfer Protocol (HTTP): This is the technology that lets you access Web pages through a Web browser.

Before the Web came along, the Internet allowed people to access and exchange print information, but all people could get were screens full of text (usually in just one font and font size). With the Web, online resources became easier to use and much more visually interesting. Five years after the Web was launched, it had more than 40 million users. Today, billions of people use the Web.

How does Tim hope people will use the Web? "Let's use the Web to create neat, new, exciting things," he says. "Let's use the Web to help people understand each other."

Tim Berners-Lee has been called one of the most influential people of the 20th century.

"The World Wide Web"—Think About It!

1. "Necessity is the mother of invention" is an old saying. Is this saying true when it comes to the invention of the Web? Explain why or why not.

____

____

____

____

____

2. Explain briefly how a computer network and the Internet are similar and different.

____

____

____

____

3. There are many advantages to the Web. For example, people can find information quickly, and they can easily connect with people around the world. What are two disadvantages of the Web?

____

____

____

____

____

Inventor Oral Presentation Outline

Choose an invention you are interested in. Research the inventor and how the invention was created. Think about how the invention has helped people or changed the world. Some ideas include

- a type of medicine such as penicillin
- transportation such as a car or an airplane
- an everyday item such as a zipper or camera

Inventor: ____

Invention: ____

Introduction Checklist

I introduced my topic in an attention-grabbing way, such as

    ❑ a quote

    ❑ a statistic

    ❑ an example

    ❑ a question

❑ I state what I am going to talk about in 1 to 3 sentences.

____

____

____

____

____

____

____

continued next page ☞

Body Checklist

❑ My main point has supporting details, examples, or descriptions.
❑ I wrote out my ideas the way I would sound if I were explaining, showing, or telling someone in person during a conversation.
❑ I read aloud what I wrote.

Tip: You do not have to use full sentences. Write it the same way you talk.

Main Point

____

____

____

Supporting Details

____

____

____

____

____

____

____

____

continued next page ☞

Conclusion Checklist

- ❑ I summarized my key points.
- ❑ I ended my oral presentation in an attention-grabbing way, such as
    - ❑ a quote
    - ❑ a statistic
    - ❑ a question

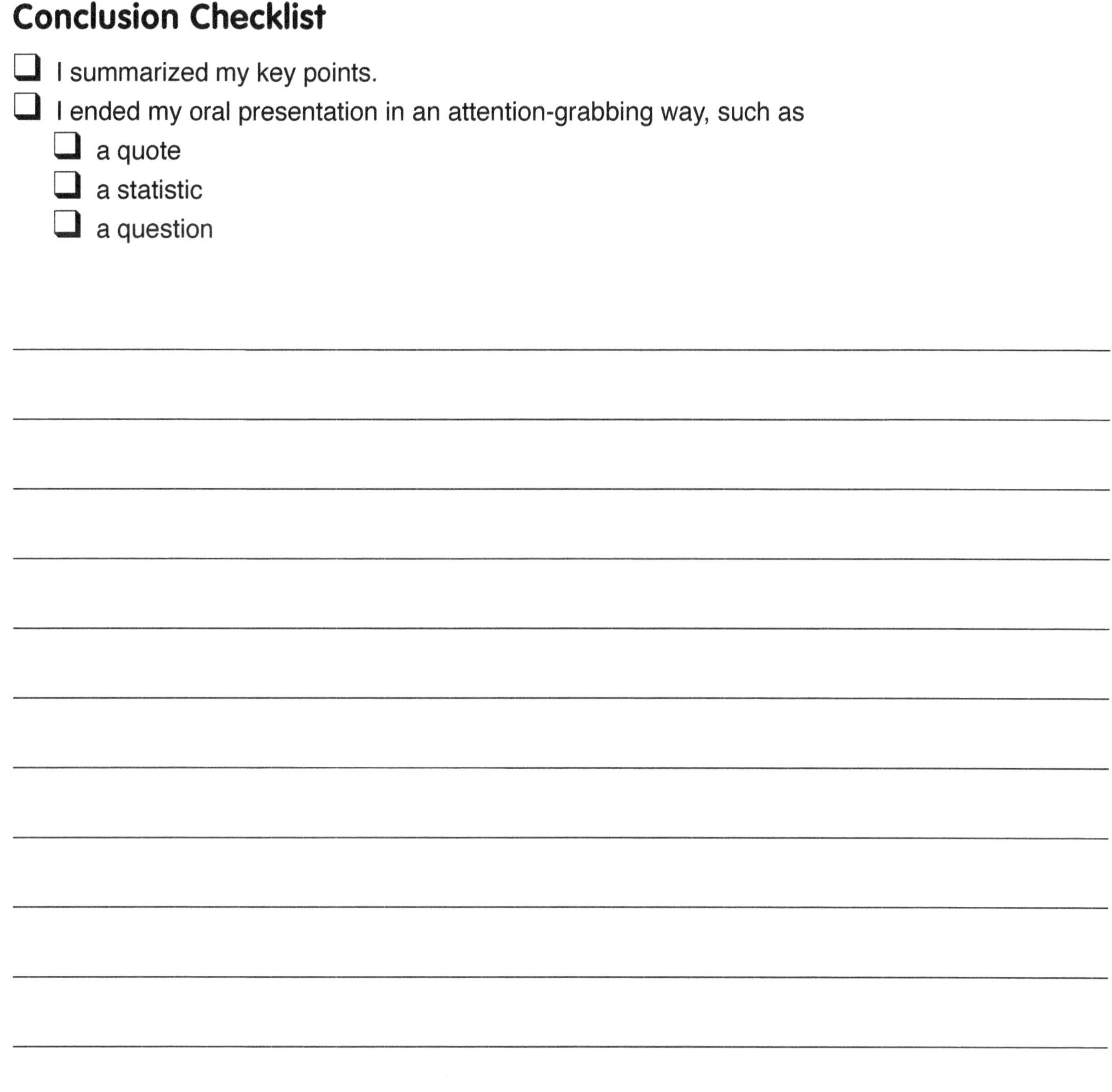

Presentation Delivery Tips

- Practice! Practice! Practice! Get comfortable with what you have written.
- Highlight your good copy in places where you would like to pause for effect, or emphasize a point.
- Think about hand gestures and making eye contact with the audience or camera.
- Think about your tone of voice to show enthusiasm, emotion, or volume.

Take One Point of View

Write an article that gives your point of view about a science-related issue. Use this outline to plan your article. Complete your work on a separate piece of paper.

A Statement of Your Point of View	
Main Idea	**Supporting Evidence**
Main Idea	**Supporting Evidence**
Main Idea	**Supporting Evidence**

STEM Rubric

	Level 1 Below Expectations	Level 2 Approaches Expectations	Level 3 Meets Expectations	Level 4 Exceeds Expectations
Knowledge of STEM Concepts	• Displays little understanding of concepts. • Rarely gives complete explanations. • Intensive teacher support is needed.	• Displays a satisfactory understanding of most concepts. • Sometimes gives appropriate, but incomplete explanations. • Teacher support is sometimes needed.	• Displays a considerable understanding of most concepts. • Usually gives complete or nearly complete explanations. • Infrequent teacher support is needed.	• Displays a thorough understanding of all or almost all concepts. • Consistently gives appropriate and complete explanations independently. • No teacher support is needed.
Application of STEM Concepts	• Relates STEM concepts to outside world with extensive teacher prompts. • Application of concepts rarely appropriate and accurate.	• Relates STEM concepts to outside world with some teacher prompts. • Application of concepts sometimes appropriate and accurate.	• Relates STEM concepts to outside world with few teacher prompts. • Application of concepts usually appropriate and accurate.	• Relates STEM concepts to outside world independently. • Application of concepts almost always appropriate and accurate.
Written Communication of Ideas	• Expresses ideas with limited critical thinking skills. • Few ideas are well organized and effective.	• Expresses ideas with some critical thinking skills. • Some ideas are well organized and effective.	• Expresses ideas with considerable critical thinking skills. • Most ideas are well organized and effective.	• Expresses ideas with in-depth critical thinking skills. • Ideas are well organized and effective.
Oral Communication of Ideas	• Rarely uses correct STEM terminology when discussing STEM concepts.	• Sometimes uses correct STEM terminology when discussing STEM concepts.	• Usually uses correct STEM terminology when discussing STEM concepts.	• Consistently uses correct STEM terminology when discussing STEM concepts.

Notes: ____

____

____

STEM Focus _______________________________

Student's Name	Knowledge of STEM Concepts	Application of STEM Concepts	Written Communication of Ideas	Oral Communication Skills	Overall Grade

STEM Expert!

Unbelievable work!

Great Work!

Keep up the effort!

Unit: Diversity of Living Things

Living Things, pages 2–3

1. Sample answer: A rabbit is a living thing because it is made up of many cells. It drinks water and eats things such as plants and grasses. It gets energy from eating and drinking so it can grow from a baby rabbit to an adult rabbit. It breathes air so it can get oxygen. It reacts to its environment by running away from animals that might eat it. Rabbits can reproduce.

2. rock: minerals; cheese: milk from a cow or goat; paper: tree; wool scarf: sheep's wool; glass jar: silica; No items are living.

3. Sample answer: Robins dig in the ground for earthworms and insects. They eat berries off bushes. They drink water from puddles.

4. Temperature is part of a habitat. A habitat provides an organism with things it needs to survive. A suitable temperature is one of those things.

Classifying Organisms, pages 4–5

1. Sample answer: It changed, because scientists discovered more about organisms. What they discovered may not have fit with the earlier system, so they changed it.

2. It is important that they use the same system, because if scientists used different classification systems, it would be difficult to share information.

3. Sample answer:

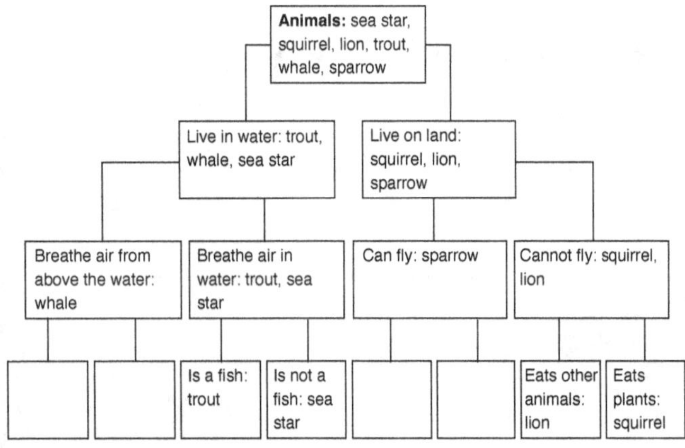

The Animal Kingdom, pages 6–7

1. A bullfrog is an animal, because it has the same characteristics as all animals: it is multicellular, eats other organisms such as flies, moves by itself, and lays eggs to reproduce.

2. Sample answer: Humans are more familiar with vertebrates, because they are easier to see.

3. They are in the same phylum, because they all have jointed legs and exoskeletons.

4. Insects have wings.

5. Sample answer:

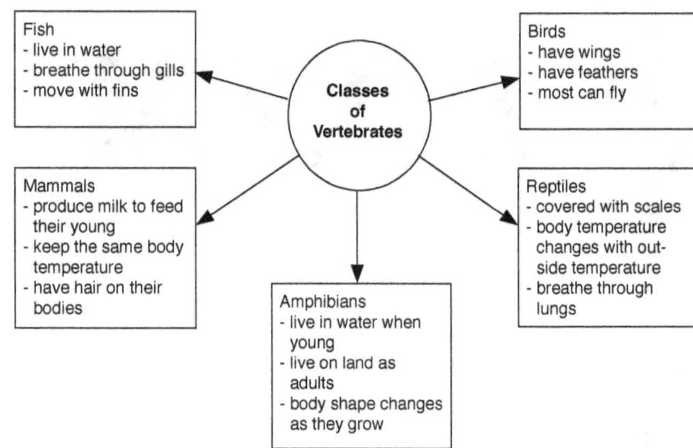

The Forgotten Kingdoms, pages 8–9

1. Sample answer:

	Cell structure	Getting nutrition	Examples of organisms	Habitat	What they do or how they affect us
Monera	- unicellular - most basic cell structure	- absorb nutrients from outside their bodies	- bacteria	- everywhere - in air, soil, water, in extreme temperatures, and in harsh chemical environments	- turn milk into cheese and yogurt - keep us healthy - make us sick - decompose waste - help make medicines
Protista	- mostly unicellular - more complex cell structure than monerans	- some make their own food - some absorb nutrients - some consume other organisms	- algae - amoebas - slime molds	- mostly in water - in damp soil - in animal bodies	- cause diarrhea and stomach upset - one causes malaria - algae are at the bottom of the food pyramid
Fungi	- mostly multicellular	- feed on dead plants and animals	- mushrooms - toadstools - mildews - molds - truffles - yeast	- most live on land in dark, moist places	- produce antibiotics - we eat some types - cause diseases in people and plants - used for baking

Cells: The Building Blocks of All Organisms, pages 10–11

1. Yes, because both are alive and carry out all of the functions of life for example, taking in nutrients, making energy, getting rid of wastes, doing tasks, and reproducing.

2. Answers will vary.

Biodiversity, pages 12–13

1. Both are classified according to characteristics and start with large groups that are divided into smaller and smaller groups.
2. Ensure that students' brochures include the worldwide locations, climate, plant and animal life, an example of a food chain, and interesting facts about their chosen biome.
3. Sketches might include a variety of deciduous trees, small bushes, and wildflowers. Animals might include deer, raccoons, foxes, and birds. Non-living features include water, air, and rocks.
4. The community I live in is similar to a habitat community, because both communities contain living and non-living things. The living things interact with each other and help each other. The living things depend on other living things for food. They also depend on non-living things for shelter, tools, and other things they need.
5. Sample answers: Humans benefit from biodiversity by getting products such as wood to build homes and furniture, and a variety of foods that can survive a range of conditions.

Species Interactions, pages 14–15

1. Corn is on the bottom because it is a plant. The mouse is next because it eats the corn. The snake is next because it eats the mouse. The hawk is at the top because it eats the snake.
2. a) Commensalism. The weed gets to spread its seeds and reproduce. The organism that carries the burrs is not affected.
   b) Mutualism. The bacteria get food. The human gets to digest food with the bacteria's help.
   c) Parasitism. The deer tick gets food, and the animal gets bitten and loses blood.
3. Sample answer: New species might kill off existing species. Organisms that ate that species would suffer and might die off, too. The invasive species might have no predators in the new area, so the population may increase rapidly. There might be so many of the invasive species that the habitat is unable to support them. Then the habitat will change and this will affect all the other organisms.

Medicine from Plants, pages 16–17

1. a) white willow tree, iii) aspirin; b) foxglove, iv) digitalis; c) fever tree, i) quinine; d) aloe, ii) alonin
2. The rubber tree does not provide us with medicine, but things such as rubber gloves and waterproof sheeting are important parts of health care and medicine.
3. For thousands of years, people have relied on plants for food, building materials, medicine, and rubber for making rubber gloves, plastic sheeting, tires, etc. The five plant parts people use are the roots, leaves, flowers, bark, and berries.
4. Rely means "to depend on something or someone."
5. Sample answer: If people do not protect the plants where they live and the plants die, we could be losing a source of potentially life-saving medicine.

Adaptations, pages 18–19

1. Sample answer: Dandelions have a long root that goes straight into the ground. This makes it difficult to pull them out. It can regrow from any root pieces left behind. Porcupines have strong claws that help them dig for food.
2. a) This keeps the alligator sheltered from hot weather.
   b) The beaver can use its front teeth underwater without swallowing water.
   c) The hippopotamus can see above the water when most of its body is hidden underwater.
3. Drawings might address adaptations related to gathering/hunting food, movement, and self-defence.

How Biodiversity Benefits Humans, pages 20–21

1. Sample categories: Food from Plants, Food from Animals, Clothing, and Medicines.
2. A farmer might plant only one type of sunflower, because it is easier to take care of one type of crop because needs are consistent. It is also easier to harvest one type of crop that matures at the same time and is the same size.
3. Growing both types of grass can make a healthy lawn, because the lawn will survive both dry and wet conditions.

Biodiversity: What Do You Think? page 22

Sample answers:

1. Plant flowers that attract bees or hummingbirds; install a bird bath.
2. Make displays about different habitats to educate others about their importance; plant native plants in the schoolyard.
3. Encourage people to plant a variety of plants that attract and support a variety of native wildlife; restore and save local habitats.
4. Plant trees along roads; create more green spaces; prevent the destruction of habitats to build roads or houses; make sure there are green spaces when new developments are built.

Biodiversity Crossword Puzzle, page 23

Across: 2. vertebrates **7.** invertebrates **10.** behavior
Down: 1. organism **3.** adaptations **4.** living **5.** cell
6. biodiversity **8.** kingdom **9.** air
Sentences: Discourage students from writing sentences that incorporate the clues. For example, organism: A plant, a squirrel, and an amoeba are all examples of an organism.

Unit: Properties of Air and Characteristics of Flight

All About Air, pages 24–25

1. Sample answer: Air can move and can move other things, as with wind. Air has a temperature, you can feel a warm

breeze. Hot air rises; upstairs is warmer on a hot day. Air can hold moisture, as on a humid day.

2. a) It warms the air in the bottle.

b) The air in the bottle expanded and moved into the balloon. I can see that the balloon inflated.

c) Air expands when heated.

d) The balloon will deflate because the air will cool and take up less space.

Taking Flight, pages 26–27

1. a) Lift, take off

b) more, drag

c) weight, land

d) Thrust, less

2. a) lift

b) weight

c) thrust

d) drag

A Short History of Flight, pages 28–29

1. Sample answer:

When	Who	Accomplishment
250	People in China	- launched unmanned hot air-balloons as military signals
1500	Leonardo da Vinci	- drew airplane-like machines
1738	Daniel Bernoulli	- stated Bernoulli's principle, which explains how wings create lift
1783	Joseph and Étienne Montgolfier	- launched the first hot-air balloon with passengers
1849	Sir George Cayley	- flew the first glider with a person onboard
1896	Otto Lilienthal	- made about 2,000 glider flights
1903	Orville and Wilbur Wright	- first to fly in a controlled and powered aircraft

Flying Through the Sky, pages 30–31

1. The flap changes the shape of the wing, so there is more drag.

2. The flaps should be flat so there will be less drag.

3. Flaps are tilted up on one wing and down on the other so that wind pushes each wing in opposite directions.

4. A bird could push the back of its wings down to increase drag and slow itself down.

5. The engine creates thrust.

Experiment: Build an Aircraft, page 32

Findings will vary. Look for evidence that students have applied and/or assessed the forces of flight on their aircraft.

Aircraft with Motors, page 33

1. Sample answer: A helicopter would be better, because it does not need a runway. A helicopter can also hover and maneuver more precisely.

Aircraft Without Motors, page 34

1. Sample answer: Direction is determined by the wind, they do not move as fast, and carry very few passengers.

2. A kite is similar to a glider, because neither has an engine, and hang-gliders are made with shapes and materials that are similar to kites.

Space Flight, pages 35–36

1. a) engine

b) air pushing up on the fuselage (minimally)

c) air passing the fuselage

d) Earth

2. Sample answer: obstacles to space travel include carrying enough food, water, and oxygen, waste disposal, effects of microgravity and radiation, boredom, and dealing with serious medical problems during the trip.

3. Sample answer: Satellites cost a lot to build, launch, and maintain. Eventually they may become dangerous when they are just obstacles in orbit and when they fall back to Earth.

Animal Fliers, page 37

1. A light skeleton helps an animal to fly, because a lighter animal has less weight to overcome when they fly.

2. Insects: can turn their wings; Bats: flap their spread-out fingers to fly; Birds: flap their wings to propel them through the air.

Furred and Finned Gliders, page 38

1. Sample answer: light materials, large wings, powerful launch device, flaps for steering

Airplanes, pages 39–40

Sample answers:

1. Pros:

- fast long-distance travel for work, vacation, and to see family

- fast delivery of parcels and medical supplies

- small airplanes are useful to some farmers

- people can visit and learn about other countries and cultures

- fly sick or injured people in remote places to a hospital

- a rewarding hobby

- help put out forest fires

- search and rescue

Cons:

- air and noise pollution that causes stress and other health problems

- germs spread quickly on planes
- animals can be scared or stressed by plane noise and vibrations
- vibrations from planes can damage buildings
- crop dusting from planes can cause chemical pollution
- chemicals used to de-ice planes pollute waterways
- security and flight delays at airports cause stress and other health problems
- planes use up lots of fossil fuel, which is a non-renewable resource
- few people survive a plane crash
- producing the materials used to build airplanes can harm the environment

2. Sample answers:
   a) They like airplane travel because their jobs depend on it.
   b) They dislike it because of the noise pollution and the health problems.
   c) They appreciate it because it allows them to spend less time traveling, and have access to distant medical services.

Flight Quiz, pages 41–42

1. lift, weight/gravity, drag, thrust
2. Air takes up space.
3. Air can be compressed.
4. Air has mass or weight.
5. a) Air that is moving quickly exerts less pressure than air that is moving more slowly. The air that is moving under the wing is moving more slowly than the air moving over the wing, so the air under the wing exerts more pressure.
   b) lift
6. It slows objects down
7. engines
8. Controlling the balance of drag on different parts of the plane helps the pilot maneuver.

Amelia Earhart, pages 43–45

1. The main idea of the article is to inform readers about the amazing bravery of Amelia Earhart, the first woman to pilot a plane across the Atlantic Ocean.
2. Amelia was the first woman to be carried across the ocean in a plane, and the first woman to fly solo across the Atlantic Ocean.
3. Answers will vary.
4. Sample answer: It means that she did not think what she did was important enough for people to make that much of a fuss about it. It shows me that she was a humble person and that she did not make things in her life bigger than they really were.
5. Answers will vary. Sample answer: Amelia and Fred might have crashed into the ocean or on an island somewhere in the Pacific Ocean.
6. Answers will vary.

Unit: Electricity

Using Electricity, pages 46–47

1. Ask students to explain their thinking. Accept any reasonable answers.
2. Sample answer: street and traffic lights, signs, home lighting, electric garden tools
3. Sample answer: cell phone, laptop computer, flashlight, portable music player, watch, smoke alarm
4. Sample answer: In a blackout, we would have to cook on the camp stove and use candles at night. We would not be able to use the radio, television, or computers. No hot water would come from the tap.

Current and Static Electricity, page 48

1. flashlight, power lines in a house, solar calculator, light switch
2. a) opposite
   b) same
3. Clothes rub together in the dryer, creating friction and building up charge. Pieces of clothing with opposite charges will stick together.

Experiment: Electric Cereal, pages 49–50

1. Expected results:
   5. a) When the comb got close to the cereal, the cereal swung to touch the comb and stuck to it.
   5. b) The cereal swung away from the comb.
   6. As the comb got closer to the cereal, the cereal moved away from the comb.
2. Friction creates a charge on the comb when it is rubbed against the wool.
3. This is static electricity since the energy does not flow along a path.
4. Test whether a comb attracts the cereal if it is not rubbed on wool, or test a different type of cereal.

Brain Stretch, page 51

The gloves would need to have some type of conductive material for you to work the touch screen. Rubber, plastic, or wool gloves would not work.

Conductors and Insulators, pages 51–52

1. Yes, it would be dangerous, because there is exposed wire and electricity can flow out of it and through the puddle to reach you.
2. Rubber handles prevent any accidentally touched electricity from flowing through the tool into the person.
3. Electricity could escape through the frayed cord, electrocuting someone.

4. Conductors: coin, stove element, safety pin, magnet, touch screen, earphone wire; Insulators: pencil, plastic button, rubber boots, glass, tires, wood table

Using Water to Produce Electricity, pages 53–54

1. a) People would be unhappy since their land will be flooded.

b) People may be happy for a new lake to use, or unhappy at the loss of the river.

c) They would be happy for the new jobs during construction.

d) They might be unhappy because of the threat of flooding if an earthquake damages the dam.

2. Answers will vary. Look for supported arguments.

Using Wind to Produce Electricity, pages 55–56

1. The lighter the blades, the less wind is needed to make them turn. A wind turbine with very light blades will be able to produce electricity when the wind is not very strong. Heavier blades require stronger wind to make them turn.

2. Mining for metal and the rocks required for concrete can pollute the environment and spoil the natural beauty of the landscape. Changing ore from the mine into metal parts for the wind turbine creates pollution. Energy is required to produce the metal parts and the concrete, and this energy may be produced in ways that create pollution.

3.

Similarities	Differences
- produce electricity - use natural, renewable sources of energy - have a turbine with blades - use a generator with moving magnets and copper coils - produce electricity	- hydroelectric power plants use the energy of moving water; wind turbines use the energy of moving air - hydroelectric power plants must be built near water; wind turbines must be in windy areas that are flat and open - wind turbines can be dangerous for flying animals; hydroelectric power plants create hazards for people and barriers to wildlife such as fish - hydroelectric dams flood large areas of land and change the flow of the river; wind turbines do not change the landforms or waterways

Transforming Energy, page 57

1. a) sound and light

b) heat

c) motion and sound

d) – f) Sample answers: computer—sound and light; flashlight—light; space heater—heat; power drill—motion

All About Electrical Circuits, pages 58–60

1. a) Parallel, because there is more than one path through which the electric current can flow.

b) Yes, because the electric current can flow past the burnt out bulb to bulb B.

2. The switch creates a gap in the circuit so electricity cannot flow through the bulb.

3. The rest of the bulbs will stay lit even when a bulb is out, and you can see which bulb is burned out.

4. a) It must be a conductor because electricity is able to get to the lightbulb to make it light up.

b) Metal, water, or a person

Life Without Electricity, pages 61–63

Sample answers: More efficient appliances can save in all cases.

a) Today: electric stove, microwave oven, toaster, kettle; Save: use another heat source such as gas

b) Today: refrigerator and freezer; Save: smaller appliances, cooler with ice, fill the freezer so it works more efficiently, do not hold the fridge door open

c) Today: lightbulbs; Save: turn off lights when not in use, use candles or gas lights

d) Today: water heater sends warm water to taps; Save: solar water heater, turn down the temperature, use less water, use an on-demand water heater

e) Today: washing machines, dryers, and electric irons; Save: wash and dry only full loads, hang to dry, cold water

f) Today: phone, emails, websites, and text messages; Save: meet in person

Electricity Crossword, page 64

Down: 1. current **2.** plastic **3.** conductor **5.** load **6.** charge **8.** glass **9.** battery

Across: 2. power **4.** insulator **7.** static **8.** generator **10.** parallel **11.** zero

Create an Electricity Game, pages 65–66

Have students play their games with a partner or in small groups.

Unit: Space

Our Sun Is a Star, page 67

1. The Sun's heat warms the earth, powers the water cycle, and creates wind. Sunlight makes plants grow, which provides us with food and oxygen.

Brain Stretch, page 67

Posters will vary. Make sure students' poster includes diagrams and labels.

Experiment: Create a Sunset, page 68

1. Light beam, maybe making some colors on the paper.
2. Reddish colors. Explanation: At sunset, the sunlight passes through much more atmosphere, so most of the blue in the sunlight is scattered. That leaves the reds and oranges to color the sunset.
3. The milky water scatters the light beam like Earth's atmoshere scatters sunlight.

Planets in Our Solar System, pages 69–71

1. 3
2. Mars has the highest-known mountain.
3. Venus is the hottest planet.
4. Mercury is the smallest planet.
5. Jupiter is the largest planet.
6. Earth is the densest.
7. Mercury has the greatest daily temperature change.
8. Uranus spins on its side.
9. a) Mercury **iii)** peppercorn
   b) Venus **v)** black bean or **vii)** pea
   c) Earth **v)** black bean or **vii)** pea
   d) Mars **vi)** kernel of corn
   e) Jupiter **ii)** gum ball or **iv)** large marble
   f) Saturn **ii)** gum ball or **iv)** large marble
   g) Uranus **i)** small number cube or **viii)** small marble
   h) Neptune **i)** small number cube or **viii)** small marble

Moons, pages 72–73

1. Diagrams should show that the Moon is in the darkest part of Earth's shadow.
2. a) From Earth, the angle at which we observe the Moon's sunlit side changes, meaning we see less or more of the Moon.
   b) The Moon phases are already in order but students may start their observation at any point along the set, affecting where #1 starts.

They Came from Outer Space, page 74

1. From largest to smallest: asteroid, meteoroid, comet.
2. Sample answer: Perseids are a group of meteors that we see streaking across the sky (like a shower) in the area where the Perseid constellation is found.

Experiment: Mass of Asteroids, page 75

1. Answers will vary.
2. metal felt heavier
3. metal weighed more
4. Metal asteroids have more mass than stone asteroids of the same size.
5. A comet contains a lot of frozen material, so it would be lighter.

Explore the Night Sky, page 76

1. a) – b) Diagrams should have a detailed title and show several starry objects.
   c) Sample answer: We looked in different directions or at different days/times.
2. a) – b) Answers will vary. Encourage students to research a culture they relate to.

Eye in the Sky, pages 77–79

1. Earth's atmosphere prevents telescopes on Earth from taking clear and detailed photos of distant objects in space. Space telescopes are outside Earth's atmosphere, so they can take clearer photos, and astronomers can learn more from these clearer photos.
2. By "serviced," the author means "fixed and improved." In the same paragraph, the author tells how space shuttle missions have "repaired, replaced, and upgraded Hubble's systems."
3. Because Mercury is so close to the Sun, Hubble would need to aim toward the Sun to take a photo of Mercury. Bright light from the Sun could damage the telescope's sensitive equipment.

Astronauts and Space Travel, pages 80–81

1. Sample answer: Food, air, and water because there is none in space; computer with photos of friends, music player, e-book reader, and Internet access for entertainment, keeping and analyzing records, and communication; therapy bands for resistance exercise; sleeping bag because blankets would not stay in place while sleeping; ear plugs to block out others' sounds; and tools to fix things.
2. Sample answer: protection from the airless, cold, radiation-filled outer space; storage for supplies (including food) and waste (dirty clothes, human waste, food packaging, etc.); exercise area; sleeping and bathroom spaces; place and equipment to perform experiments; communication with Earth; windows.

Other Spacecraft, pages 82–83

1. Sample answer: Orbiters have no danger of crash-landing and no need to launch to leave the planet. They do not need to withstand conditions or terrain on the planet. Landers can take samples and examine the planet on a microscopic level.
2. Sample answer: Rovers have to withstand fast acceleration, high and low temperatures, pressure, and dust, and must function without repair. They must be small enough and light enough to fit on a spacecraft and there has to be a way to remove them from the spacecraft when they reach their destination. The rover should be remotely controlled, move over the landscape, and send pictures.
3. A rover can move to get more or better samples or to take pictures from different angles.

Astronaut Research Report, page 84
Have students share their reports with the class.

Space Technology, pages 85–87
1.–3. Answers will vary. Look for reasoned arguments.
4. a) Fresh **vi)** Food is not preserved so it must be eaten quickly.
   b) Intermediate Moisture **ii)** Food with some water removed; water is not replaced before eating.
   c) Irradiated **iii)** Food is cooked and packed in foil pouches. It is sterilized by radiation so it can be kept at room temperature.
   d) Natural **v)** Food is ready to eat and stored in flexible pouches.
   e) Rehydratable **i)** Food is freeze-dried to remove water. Water is replaced before eating.
   f) Thermostabilized **iv)** Food is heated to kill bacteria so it can be stored at room temperature.
5. Answers will vary.

Animals in Space—Fair or Not? page 88
1. Any reasoned answer is acceptable.

Those Puzzling Planets, pages 89–90
Across: 2. moon **4.** orbit **5.** Mars **7.** Saturn **10.** Earth
11. Neptune **13.** Uranus **14.** Mercury **17.** Sun **18.** asteroids
Down: 1. solar system **3.** constellation **6.** comet **8.** meteor
9. Venus **12.** Jupiter **15.** Canadarm **16.** galaxy

What Does an Engineer Do? pages 93–94
1. Answers will vary. Have some students share with the class.
2. Sample answer: Engineers make things, build things, and fix things that people use every day.

Incredible Bionics, pages 100–103
1. A hearing aid is an example of a bionic device because it is created by humans, and it improves the function of a body part (the ear).
2. An organ created with a 3-D printer does not function like a human organ.
3. Answers will vary. Sample answer: Yes, it would be useful for the two kinds of scientists to share discoveries. For example, both kinds of scientists might be working on creating artificial arms and legs that function like human limbs, or bionic eyes that help people see and help robots sense the world around them.

The World Wide Web, pages 104–106
1. The saying is true for the invention of the Web. Sample answer: First, Tim had a need to find an easier way to access information on computers that were connected to his computer. This need led him to invent the Web as an easier way for computers to share information.
2. Answers may vary. Sample answer: A computer network and the Internet are similar because they both connect things and they both allow people to share information. They are different because a computer network connects individual computers, and the Internet connects networks of computers.
3. Answers will vary. Sample answers: Anyone can publish information on the Web, and the information they publish might not be accurate. Some people use the Web for cyber-bullying. Others use the Web to spread computer viruses. People can use the Web to hack into computers and steal information.